ARMOUR'S
ALMANAC

ARMOUR'S ALMANAC

or

Around the Year in 365 Days

by RICHARD ARMOUR

With timely illustrations
by Campbell Grant

McGRAW-HILL BOOK COMPANY, INC.

New York   Toronto   London

Armour's Almanac

Library of Congress Catalog Card Number: 61-14346

First Edition   02253

Author's Note

The reader who for some unaccountable reason wishes to verify the facts in this book is urged to spend his evenings in the stacks of a well-stocked library, if possible in the company of a well-stacked librarian. The stickler may still get stuck, but he will have learned that much of what is said in this book is true and the rest might as well be.

R.A.

JANUARIUS

J ANUARY *is named after Janus, a two-faced god who could look backward and forward at the same time. It took him twice as long as the other gods to get ready for work in the morning, since he had two faces to wash. Also he found it uncomfortable to sleep on his back. But there were advantages. For instance, the gods felt more relaxed when he was on sentry duty. In addition to giving his name to January, it was Janus who coined the expression, "I don't know whether I'm coming or going."*

1 Betsy Ross, who made the first American flag, was born on January 1, 1752. She sewed together red, white, and blue pieces of her skirt, blouse, and petticoat. By the time she had made five or six flags, her wardrobe was exhausted, and tourists gathered to peer through her windows, as they still do today. George Washington had his heart set on six-pointed stars, but Betsy persuaded him to make them five-pointed, saying they looked better, but really wanting to save a little sewing.

2 On January 2, 1859, *The Dime Book of Practical Etiquette* was published by Erastus F. Beadle. Although it was not a dime novel, because of lack of plot, it was novel and sold for a dime. Mr. Beadle was concerned about the manners of Americans, as well he might be, for in 1859 there was a noticeable lack of refinement. After reading Mr. Beadle's book, however, people remembered to put their toothpicks in their pockets after using them, instead of letting them hang from their lips while speaking, as they were later to do with cigarettes. If people belched less often and less loudly in public, this may be attributed to improvement in diet rather than etiquette. After the death of Mr. Beadle, Emily Post took over. She contributed greatly to raising the standards of etiquette and the price of etiquette books.

3 This is the day devoted to St. Genevieve, the patron saint of Paris. Her prayers are said to have averted attack on the city by Attila the Hun. It is interesting to conjecture what effect they would have, if she were now living, on the average American tourist. We also wonder what the good saint would think of the Folies Bergère, the can-can, Left Bank artists, and other manifestations of life in Paris today. It is quite possible she would regret having been so hasty about Attila.

4   On January 4, 1885, Mary Gartside, aged twenty-two, of Davenport, Iowa, became the first person in the United States to have her appendix removed. She was a lucky young woman, not only because she lived through the operation but because, bathing suits being what they were in 1885, she was able to go swimming the next summer without having to worry that the scar would show.

5   This day is dedicated to St. Simeon Stylites, the patron saint of flagpole sitters. In Syria, in the fifth century, he lived on a pillar 60 feet high and 3 feet across, staying up there thirty years without ever once coming down. (No spotlight being kept on him at night, we can only assume that there was no cheating.) Apparently he loved the open air and had no fear of height, even when he looked over the edge. Exercise must have been something of a problem, since there was room only for deep knee bends. We are told, however, that by preaching from atop the pillar he "exercised a great influence," and he must also have kept up the muscle tone of his vocal cords.

Prince Wilhelm of Sweden arrived in New York City on January 5, 1927, to become the first lecturer of royal blood to speak for personal profit. Although his thick accent made him impossible to understand, he was applauded vigorously.

6 On January 6, 1640, the Virginia General Assembly
ordered half the tobacco crop burned. This was not
because of any puritanical objection to the weed, but because a surplus had driven prices so low that planters faced
ruin. During the crop burning, many farmers cannily hung
hams out in their back yards, and Virginia tobacco-smoked
ham was something special that year.

7 Fannie Farmer published her first cookbook on January 7, 1896. Since her books have been followed re-
ligiously by so many housewives, it is no wonder they have
sold almost as well as the Bible. Known as "The Mother
of Level Measurements," she disclaimed authorship of the
famous line, "It takes a heaping spoonful to make a house
a home."

The Panama Canal was successfully navigated on January 7, 1914, inaugurating a new era. Begun under the
administration of Teddy Roosevelt, it was also called the
Big Ditch, and the first failure of an oversize ship to get
through was laughingly known as the Big Stick. Henceforth
the United States was to enjoy better maritime transportation and always to be at the point of war with the Republic
of Panama.

8 On this day in 1882 Oscar Wilde, the English poet
and playwright, appeared at a reception in New
York clad in a black velvet jacket, black knee breeches, and
long black stockings. The invitation had said simply "black
tie," but Oscar was the sort who always did things up brown
or, in this instance, black. Add to all this a sunflower as
big as a saucer in his buttonhole, and you can see why he
made the list of the Ten Most Outlandishly Dressed Men
of 1882.

Larger crowds than ever

9 It was on January 9, 1873 that the Rev. Henry Ward
Beecher, one of the most popular preachers of the
time, was charged once too often with adultery. In the suit
brought against him by Theodore Tilton for alienation of
his wife's affections, there was a miscarriage of justice and
the jury was hung. The Rev. Beecher, however, escaped un-
scathed, and on Sundays drew larger crowds than ever, especially when he preached on Sin.

10 On January 10, 1928, Leon Trotsky, who had been
voted the Communist Most Likely to Succeed
Lenin, was exiled to Kazakstan. Early the next year he was
banished from Russia. He was told he could live any-
where, but not how long. In 1940, in a suburb of Mexico
City, he was killed by a man who happened by with a
pickaxe. Some thought Stalin had a hand in this, but the
District Attorney of Mexico City had trouble subpoenaing
him. Things might have been different had Trotsky remained in Russia. For instance, he would probably have
been killed sooner.

11 The first life insurance company in the United States was chartered on January 11, 1759. Founded in Philadelphia, it was called the Corporation for the Relief of Poor and Distressed Widows and Children of Presbyterian Ministers. Payments were kept low on the theory that the wives and children of Presbyterian ministers were used to being poor and distressed and there was no point in their suddenly beginning to live better when the old man died.

On January 11, 1878, a Brooklyn milkman, Alexander Campbell, began delivering milk in glass bottles, instead of ladling it out of a pail. An advantage of the milk bottle was that notes could now be left for the milkman, which previously had not been either possible or necessary. Contrary to general belief, most of these notes are businesslike rather than amatory, though milkmen have become skilled in deciphering difficult handwriting, just in case.

12 Dr. H. L. Smith, a professor of astronomy at Davidson College, made the first X-ray photograph in the United States on January 12, 1896. Dr. Smith was tired of looking through a telescope at the stars and wanted to see something close at hand. By coincidence, it was the hand of a corpse that he X-rayed, first firing a bullet into it and then taking a picture to see if the bullet was there. It was there, all right, though there is no explanation of why it didn't go on through. Can you think of anything more gruesome than a photo of a bullet in a second-hand hand?

13 Salmon P. Chase, Lincoln's Secretary of the Treasury and later Chief Justice of the U.S. Supreme Court, was born on January 13, 1808. Among his other distinctions, he is remembered as the only Chief Justice named after a fish. He proved conclusively that you can rise to high place, no matter what you are named, provided you get through boyhood. It must be remembered, however, that Chief Justice is an appointive office, and whether a Salmon could ever have been elected President is open to question.

That nostalgic urge

Stephen Foster, the famous author of American folk songs, died on January 13, 1864. His best-loved song is "My Old Kentucky Home," which gives people a nostalgic urge to return to Kentucky, especially if they have never been there.

14 The name "celluloid," describing a substance made of cellulose and oid, was registered on January 14, 1873, but it was not until July that the first celluloid collar wilted in public and made the wearer wish he had stayed home and sat around in his underwear.

On January 14, 1914, Henry Ford inaugurated the assembly line, reducing the time of putting a car together from twelve and a half hours to only ninety-three minutes. By making automobiles cheap enough for anyone to own, this contributed significantly to traffic accidents, Mr. Ford's bank account, smog, and the agility of pedestrians.

15 On this day in 1899 Edwin Markham, a California schoolteacher, published his poem, "The Man with the Hoe." He did not realize that schoolteachers are supposed to assign poems, not write them.

16 It was on January 16, 1599 that Edmund Spenser, the author of *The Faerie Queene*, died. *The Faerie Queene* is one of the longest poems in the English language, and seems even longer. At his death, this great Elizabethan poet had achieved all of his ambitions, except (1) to live until 1600 and (2) to be thought the author of Shakespeare's plays. Spenser's name is often spelled "Spencer" by students who write on examinations about William Wadsworth and Samuel Peeps.

France made the first move toward recognizing the independence of the United States on January 16, 1778. Americans sometimes forget that without this recognition they might have lost the Revolutionary War and still be British, with stiff mustaches, protruding teeth, rolled umbrellas, and hyphenated last names.

17 This is the Feast of Anthony the Great. Anthony, an Egyptian monk, was a skinny ascetic, and it would be more appropriate to honor him by dieting once a year than by gorging.

The ceremony of Wassailing the Apple Trees is observed on January 17 in Carhampton, Somerset. Men of the village make the rounds of the orchards at night, carrying a pail of cider, singing like mad, and now and then firing a gun through the branches to scare off evil spirits. The purpose is said to be "to insure the health of the fruit trees," though not even Lloyd's of London would insure the health of the wassailers, out there stumbling around in the dark with a pail of cider in one hand and a shotgun in the other, blazing away at anything that looks like an evil spirit. Come apple-picking time, about the only able-bodied villagers are the women and children.

Captain James Cook on January 17, 1779, named the Sandwich Islands after Lord Sandwich, head of the British Admiralty. Captain Cook was obviously bucking for a promotion and would surely have been made an admiral had he not been slain by islanders who were incensed at the thought of being called Sandwiches. Subsequently the Sandwich Islands came to be known as the Hawaiian Islands, which was a severe blow to local humorists.

18 On January 18, 1943, during World War II, bakers throughout the United States were directed to stop selling sliced bread for the duration. The purpose of this was to save manpower, needed for slicing Germans. Many patriotic Americans uncomplainingly cut their own bread, realizing that war calls for all sorts of sacrifices.

19 The first regular transatlantic radio broadcast was sent on January 19, 1903, between Cape Cod, Massachusetts, and Cornwall, England. Greetings were exchanged between President Theodore Roosevelt and King Edward VII. President Roosevelt, who had spent a good deal of time in the West, and was rough and ready, shouted,

Exchanged greetings

in code, "Howdy, Ed." King Edward, carried away by the excitement of this historic occasion, exclaimed, "Good show!"

On January 19, 1949, Congress raised the salary of the President of the United States from $75,000 to $100,000, with a $50,000 tax-free expense allowance. The Presidency not being unionized, shorter hours and better working conditions were not mentioned.

20 This is St. Agnes' Eve, when maids of old, and especially old maids of old, prayed for husbands. It is not known what bachelors did. Some probably got drunk with the boys; others left town for a few days. One, in Keats's poem, hid in his girl friend's closet and watched her undress. Apparently satisfied with what he saw, he carried her off and perhaps eventually married her, though Keats indicates only that they lived together happily ever after.

21 On January 21, 1919, some 35,000 New York garment workers began a successful strike for a forty-four-hour week. However, employers lost nothing, because the shorter work week was offset by shorter skirts, and as many garments were produced as ever.

22 The first American novel, *The Power of Sympathy*, was published in Boston on January 22, 1789. Establishing a pattern for American novelists, it dealt with such themes as seduction, incest, and suicide. Few eyebrows were raised in Boston, however, since they were already as high as they would go.

23 This day is devoted to the memory of St. Ildefonsus. Keep him in mind, if you can remember the name.

Édouard Manet, the French painter, was born on January 23, 1832. As the leader of the Impressionists, he made quite an impression on everyone. Starting with Manet, paintings began to look less and less like what they looked like. The art lover could get the effect better by standing across the room and squinting his eyes or, better yet, closing them completely. Manet is sometimes confused with Monet, another French Impressionist, because they both wore black berets.

Eleanora Duse, the Italian tragedienne, made her American debut on January 23, 1893, playing the title role in *Camille*. The audience cried throughout the play, and when it was over cried again, this time: "Duse! Duse! Duse!" (Not to be confused with "Duce! Duce! Duce!") They would not leave the theater until she bowed and waved her hands to prove that she had not really died of consumption.

24 Gold was discovered on the property of John A. Sutter, in California, on January 24, 1848. This led to the Gold Rush and the Forty-niners. Sutter himself was a Forty-eighter and in no hurry. But squatters moved in and sat all over his property, so close to each other that he was afraid to swing a pick, despite all that gold under there. He would have been better off if he had not owned the place and had come around the Horn like everyone else.

This was the momentous day, in 1899, when Humphrey O'Sullivan, of Lowell, Massachusetts, patented the rubber heel.

25 This is St. Paul's Day. It is an old belief that sun on St. Paul's Day means a good year. One thing is sure: it means a good, sunny day.

26 On January 26, 1838, Tennessee became the first state to enact a prohibition law. The measure was "an act to repeal all laws licensing tippling houses," some of which looked to patrons as if they were not only tippling but toppling. The net effect of the law was to increase the amount of illegal drinking. The gross effect was, well, gross.

27 Charles Lutwidge Dodgson, an English clergyman and mathematician, was born on January 27, 1832. This would be nothing to get excited about except that Dodgson was also Lewis Carroll, who wrote *Alice in Wonderland, Through the Looking Glass,* and *An Elementary Treatise on Determinants.* It is interesting that Dodgson, who wrote books for children, remained a bachelor all his life. This way, he could write without always being interrupted, and keep all the royalties for himself.

28 The marriage of King Henry VII of England (born on January 28, 1457) to Elizabeth of York ended the Wars of the Roses, and just in time, for everyone's garden was a mess.

Everyone's garden was a mess

29 On January 29, 1889, Crown Prince Rudolph of Austria-Hungary, heir to the Hapsburg crown, killed his mistress and then took his own life in a hunting lodge at Mayerling, Austria. This is the sort of thing that historical novels and popular musicals are made of. Killing a mistress is considered romantic, while killing a wife is considered murder.

30 On January 30, 1933, Adolf Hitler became Chancellor of Germany. When saluting him, his followers said, "Heil Hitler," and Hitler responded with "Heil Hitler" and sometimes "Heil Me" without the slightest embarrassment.

There seems to be no connection between Hitler's being named Chancellor of Germany and the beginning, also on January 30, 1933, of the radio program "The Lone Ranger."

31 If the weather was miserable today, it may not help any to know that the forecast is for worse during February. "If winter comes, can spring be far behind?" asked Shelley, who had a calendar and should have known without asking. Eventually someone told him, and he lost no time moving from England to Italy.

FEBRUARIUS

FEBRUARY gets its name from a Roman festival of purification that was held on the fifteenth of the month. The festival was a great success, most Romans eating and drinking themselves into a stupor. However, a few purer-than-thou types, like the Vestal Virgins, would have no part of it. In the original Roman calendar February was the last month of the year, preceding January. What was gained by the shift is anybody's guess.

1 On February 1, 1898, Dr. Truman J. Martin, a physician of Buffalo, New York, became the first holder of an automobile insurance policy. Of a somewhat conservative nature, he played it safe and took out complete coverage, including compensation for damage from sandstorms, on which the premium was very reasonable in Buffalo. One thing was sure—with Dr. Martin at the wheel there would be no annoying wait for an M.D. if he ran over a pedestrian.

2 This is Ground Hog Day, and anyone who has ever eaten ground hog, which is something like ground round, will never forget it. If you look into a mirror and see shadows under your eyes, there will be six more weeks of winter, though you may not think you will live that long.

The first movie close-up was made on February 2, 1893, by a cameraman employed by Thomas A. Edison. It showed comedian Fred Ott in the process of sneezing, which explains all those little spots on the film.

3 The Sixteenth Amendment, establishing the income tax, became the law of the land on February 3, 1913. One of the most important effects of the income tax was on family life, the wife and children now becoming known as dependents and having a certain money value. An equally popular feature, had it ever been adopted, would have been to permit a man to take off so much a year for depreciation, until he could write himself off completely.

4 This is the birth date, in 1802, of Mark Hopkins, the pioneer American educator. President James A. Garfield once said that education could be improved if you had Mark Hopkins sitting on one end of a log and a stu-

Higher education

dent on the other. Presumably they would be facing toward the middle, though for independent study they might face outward. Although Garfield's educational plan received little support, he is credited with having invented the teeter-totter.

5 The push-key adding machine was patented on February 5, 1850. People who never could add were now as useful as anybody, as long as they pushed the right buttons. Some worriers, the kind who climb into a refrigerator to see whether the light really goes off when the door closes, insisted on adding up the figures themselves, just to check. For them, it must be admitted that the adding machine was no time saver.

On February 5, 1937, President Franklin D. Roosevelt urged Congress to enlarge the Supreme Court. Some people call this "court packing," which sounds worse and is meant to. Congress denied FDR his request, and he was forced to sit around and wait for conservative justices to die off. They did, but with exasperating slowness.

6 On this day in 1900 Theodore Roosevelt, mentioned as a possible running mate with William McKinley on the Republican ticket, issued the following statement: "Under no circumstances could I or would I accept the nomination for the Vice Presidency." Four months later he accepted the nomination. This is the sort of thing a man hates to be reminded of.

7 Charles Dickens was born on February 7, 1812. There is a striking resemblance between the career of this great English novelist and that of David Copperfield. We can only surmise that if the author had been named David Copperfield, he would have written a novel called *Charles Dickens*. This is only a conjecture, of course, but we find it fascinating.

8 Mary, Queen of Scots, was beheaded on February 8, 1587, on a charge of plotting the murder of Queen Elizabeth. She dressed in crimson silk, it being less likely to show stains. Queen Elizabeth was always having someone's head chopped off, and a substantial part of the royal budget went for axe wielders, knife sharpeners, and head holders. She was convinced that capital punishment was a deterrent to crime, at least insofar as the person executed was concerned.

9 The U.S. Weather Bureau was authorized on February 9, 1870, to provide a central agency to which to address complaints. At first it was called the Weather Department, but the name was changed to Weather Bureau to make it easier to operate under a bureaucracy. Some thought it should be called the Whether Bureau, since it was supposed to know whether it would rain tomorrow.

On February 9, 1861, Jefferson Davis was elected President of the Confederacy. If the South had won the war, we would now have Davis's Birthday, the Davis Memorial, the Davis Tunnel, Davis pennies, etc. As it is, all we have is the Davis Cup, and the Australians usually have that.

10 The Mormons, under the leadership of Brigham Young, left Illinois on February 10, 1846, in search of new territory in which to settle. Before they set out, each man filled his wagon with enough food and water, and a sufficient number of wives, to last until the next stop. When they reached Utah, Brigham Young made the famous remark: "This is the place." He also said, though this is less quoted: "Pile out."

11 On this day, in 1808, anthracite coal was burned as a fuel for the first time in the U.S. by Judge Jesse Fell, in his home at Wilkes-Barre, Pennsylvania. Coal is formed as the result of decomposition of vegetable matter, but it takes so long that there is no use standing around and waiting.

Thomas Alva Edison, the great inventor, was born in Milan on February 11, 1847. It was a lucky break for the United States that it was Milan, Ohio.

12 James Oglethorpe founded the city of Savannah, Georgia, on February 12, 1733. Here is how the city got its name. A farmhouse and barn caught fire one night, and the farmer barely escaped with his life. Still in the flaming house was the rest of the farmer's family, and in the barn was his livestock. Neighbors who came to the rescue heard the distraught farmer call out in anguish, "Save Anna! Save Anna!" Not until someone risked his life to enter the blazing building and rescue the farmer's wife was it realized that her name was Mary. Anna was a prize heifer. The farmer was inconsolable, but the city of Savannah got a name.

13 On February 13, 1741, Andrew Bradford of Philadelphia published the first magazine in America. It also held the distinction of being the first magazine to suspend publication, which it did after three issues. The magazine might have survived with a few advertisements for automobiles, perfumes, hair tonics, and depilatories. But in those days people traveled by horse, smelled like people (or horses), and neither encouraged nor discouraged the growth of hair.

14 Thomas Robert Malthus, the British political economist, was born on February 14, 1766. According to Happy Tom's forecast, you would never have been born, or at best would be dying of slow starvation. It was his belief that increasing population must inevitably outstrip the available food supply. But since the population of the world has doubled since Malthus wrote his book, something has obviously gone wrong. If he were alive today, he would be terribly embarrassed and try to shift the blame to agricultural methods and transportation and the fad for dieting. Or, still being hopeful, he might say, "Just wait!"

This is St. Valentine's Day. Dedicated to love, it is a day when all sorts of touching, sentimental things happen. For instance, there was the St. Valentine's Day Massacre, on February 14, 1929, when seven members of the O'Bannion gang, rivals of the Al Capone gang, were machine-gunned in a Chicago garage. At the funeral, each casket was tastefully decorated with a horseshoe-shaped Good Luck floral piece, and the mourners sang "Hail, Hail, the Gangs Are All Here." There wasn't a dry throat in the place.

15 On February 15, 1764, St. Louis, Missouri, was established as a fur-trading post. Women who didn't like the furs they had been given for Christmas could come in and trade them for others. Not until the Revolution, a dozen years later, were there comparable scenes of violence.

Adhesive postage stamps were introduced on February 15, 1842, in New York City. Now people had a useful, rather than spiteful, reason to stick out their tongues.

16 It was on this day, in 1862, that General U. S. Grant won his nickname of "Unconditional Surrender" because of the harsh terms he conveyed to the troops in Fort Donelson, a Confederate stronghold. Grant himself had received harsher terms, such as "boozer," from the Confederates—and anyhow, doesn't "Unconditional Surrender" seem a little long for a nickname?

On February 16, 1868, a group known as the "Jolly Corks" organized themselves into the Benevolent and Protective Order of Elks, changing their initials from J.C. to B.P.O.E. In some chapters, the elk's head on the wall has cork-tipped antlers, in memory of the good old days.

The Franco-Prussian War ended on or about February 16, 1871, with the defeat of Franco.

17 On February 17, 1876, the first sardine was canned, at Eastport, Maine. Moments later, the second sardine was canned, and then another and another, until the sardines in the can were packed in there like sardines.

The first exhibition of Modern Art was shown in New York on February 17, 1913. There were works by Picasso, Matisse, and other famous artists, but Duchamp's "Nude Descending a Staircase" got most of the attention. What aroused popular interest was the idea of a woman on her way downstairs, having forgotten to put her clothes on. Had she been *ascending* the stairs, heading for bed, there wouldn't have been so much of a stir.

18 February 18, 1678, marked the publication of Bunyan's *Pilgrim's Progress*. Because of all the walking its hero did, a more appropriate title might have been *Pilgrim's Bunyan's Progress*. Anyhow, it's a great book and a force for good, as people frequently say who haven't read it.

The French explorer La Salle established the first settlement in Texas on February 18, 1685. In a ten-gallon *chapeau*, La Salle looked every inch a Texan, but he never could make "Bonjour, Monsieur" sound like "Howdy, pardner."

Every inch a Texan

19 According to a reputable source, at a dinner party in New York on February 19, 1910, "Diamond Jim" Brady ate seven dozen oysters, five servings of roast beef, and two gallons of stewed fruit, all of which he washed down with three gallons of orange juice. As he pushed himself back from the table, Diamond Jim muttered something which reporters were unable to catch, perhaps because of the clatter made as the table and dishes crashed to the floor. But it could have been, "I'm full."

20 The Federal postal system was established on February 20, 1792, and postmen started on their rounds, leaving letters and packages in mailboxes and now and then a hunk of flesh in the mouth of someone's dog.

The postal system established

21 On February 21, 1878, the first telephone directory was published, in New Haven, Connecticut. There were only fifty names, and the directory was too thin to be of much use as a doorstop, a pants presser, or a way of raising up a small child at the dinner table.

22 This is Washington's Birthday. George Washington was born on February 22, 1732. He was to become famous for chopping down a cherry tree, never telling a lie, and throwing a dollar (a silver dollar—even George couldn't have done it with a dollar bill) across a river. It is probably because of his carelessness with money that banks close on his birthday, as a warning.

But what is really important about February 22 is that on

this day in 1923 the first successful chinchilla farm in the United States was established in Los Angeles.

23 Emma Willard, a pioneer in education for women, was born on February 23, 1787. More significant than her contribution to education was the fact that she wrote the words to "Rocked in the Cradle of the Deep," a famous song full of high thoughts and low notes. In time, Mrs. Willard became reconciled to the fact that it would never be chosen as the Alma Mater song of Emma Willard School, the girls' school of which she was the founder.

The siege of the Alamo began on February 23, 1836. Remember the Alamo?

24 It was on February 24, 1868, that the House of Representatives resolved to impeach President Andrew Johnson for "high crimes and misdemeanors." The Senate failed by one vote to convict. When the vote was announced, President Johnson was overjoyed. One of those who congratulated him was, however, biting his lips and holding back the tears. It was the President of the Senate, Ben Wade, who was next in line. Think of it, one measly vote!

The infamous French "Bluebeard" was executed at Versailles on this date in 1922. He had murdered ten of his thirteen fiancées, afterward burning their bodies. There was a tidy streak in him.

25 On February 25, 1836, Samuel Colt patented the six-shooter. This is a revolver containing six bullets, which only in movies or TV westerns can be shot seven or eight times without reloading. It has been a great help to bandits, bank robbers, and players of Russian roulette.

26 On this day in 1815, Napoleon escaped from Elba.
In the next Hundred Days the busy little fellow entered Paris, fought and lost at Waterloo, and was exiled to St. Helena. In a sense, though, all he did was move from one island to another.

27 On February 27, 1873, as the result of a financial scandal, the House of Representatives voted to censure two members for having accepted favors. It is no wonder the members of the House were incensed. Until the thing blew over, and the public forgot, they were going to have to scrape along on their Congressional salaries and allowances. It looked like hard times for a few weeks. In the cadenced words of the motion of censure: "You guys gotta be more careful."

Republicans

28 At a political meeting in Ripon, Wisconsin, in 1854, the name "Republican" was adopted to describe the principles of what was subsequently to be known as the Republican Party. No one thinking to check in a dictionary, they were not aware that a republican is "Any of certain birds that nest in communities, esp. the cliff swallow and the African sociable weaverbird." Fortunately for the Republicans, the Democrats never found out about that "African sociable weaverbird" business, either.

29 In leap year, which comes every four years from an accumulation of hours, this extra day is added. It seems a messy way to patch up the calendar, but that's how it is. During leap year, women come right out and propose to men, while in an ordinary look-before-you-leap year they have to make a man think it was his own idea. According to one authority, "Leap year is more properly known as *bissextile*," which is the name for a year with 366 days. But even this, you will notice, has sex in it. It's something you just can't get away from, no matter how learned you are.

MARTIUS

MARCH, *called* Martius *by the Romans, got its name from Mars, the god of war. It was considered a propitious time to start fighting, provided you out-numbered the enemy. March was the first month of the year until 46 B.C., when Julius Caesar, who had to do something to get his mind off Cleopatra, started messing around with the calendar. It continued to be the beginning of the legal year in England until 1752, the English not wishing to make a change hastily. March, we are told, comes in like a lion and goes out like a lamb, or vice versa, having a weakness for impersonations and quick changes of costume.*

1 It was on March 1, 1812, that Byron casually penned the words, "I awoke one morning and found myself famous." It must be doubted, however, that he found himself famous immediately on awakening, unless he was sleepwalking down the middle of the Strand. More likely, since it was the success of the first two cantos of *Childe Harold's Pilgrimage* that turned the trick, it was only after getting up and stretching and padding over to the door, under which was a note from his publisher saying: "You are famous. Everybody is watching you. For God's sake, behave yourself!"

2 On this date in 1836, Mexico declared its independence from Texas. No, it was the other way around.

3 Ludwig van Beethoven's Piano Sonata in C Sharp Minor was published on March 3, 1802. Most people know it as the "Moonlight Sonata," although many think of it as "Our Song." It was dedicated by Beethoven to the Countess Julie Guicciardi, perhaps in the hope that it would melt her down, but she remained unmolten.

4 John Adams was inaugurated President of the United States on March 4, 1797. He was the first Chief Executive to reside in the White House in Washington, having previously lived at various places, including the Union Tavern in Georgetown. Eyewitnesses say he left the Tavern reluctantly, and a little unsteadily, waving a tankard of ale and coining that timeless remark: "I shall return."

Another President, Benjamin Harrison, on March 4, 1889, became the first grandson of a President to become President. This is the sort of information that is indispensable in crossword puzzles and quizzes, and we shall try to supply more of it.

Drank from his fingerbowl

On this day in 1896 a visiting rajah drank from his fingerbowl at a state dinner given by Queen Victoria. To prevent embarrassment, the Queen sipped at her own, and the guests did likewise. Actually, it is suspected that the rajah knew better, since he later dipped his fingers into his tea, and slyly looked up at the Queen.

5 On March 5, 1934, Mother-in-Law Day was first celebrated in Amarillo, Texas. It was during the Depression, and a mother-in-law was a mighty popular woman if she owned a house and you could move in with her. As economic conditions improved, things reverted to normal, and Mother-in-Law Day has been celebrated only sporadically ever since.

6 Michelangelo Buonarroti, the Italian sculptor, was born on March 6, 1475. He is usually called Michelangelo for short, though Mike would be even shorter. Since he lived before the age of specialization and of unions, he was not only a sculptor but a painter, architect, engineer, and poet. No wonder he had difficulty filling out questionnaires when he came to "Occupation."

7 On March 7, 1908, the mayor of Cincinnati told the city council that no woman was physically fit to operate an automobile. Some member of the council apparently leaked the mayor's remarks, for that night, as he entered his home, his wife hit him over the head with a bronze bust which it later took two men to lift and replace on the hall table. The man who was elected to fill out the mayor's unexpired term kept his opinions to himself.

8 On this day in 1765 the British House of Lords passed the infamous Stamp Act. The colonists had to put stamps on all the paper they used, even paper towels, paper napkins, and paper hats at parties. The British repealed the Stamp Act in 1766, but the damage was already done: the colonists could never forget the taste of mucilage. It is a wonder they waited another ten years before starting the Revolution.

Along about now comes National Smile Week, a period when some people lock themselves indoors and draw the blinds.

9 Charles Graham of New York City is revered by dentists for having come up with some workable, if primitive, artificial teeth on March 9, 1822. Those who found them inadequate for coping with corn on the cob at a dinner party could always rise quickly from the table, break into a spirited flamenco, and use their dental plates as castanets.

Never anything like this

On March 9, 1830, a rainfall of small herring almost deluged the tiny island of Ula, off the coast of Scotland. Previously, it had rained cats and dogs, but never anything like this. Most people stayed indoors, listening to the pitter-patter of herring on the roof. But some stood in the street, open-mouthed with amazement, and now and then a herring found its mark. There has never been a completely satisfactory explanation for the incident; all the local fishermen know is that for a while the herring market was shot to hell.

10 On March 10, 1775, Daniel Boone and a company of frontiersmen were hired by the Transylvania Company to cut a road through the wilderness to the Kentucky River. As soon as Dan'l bought himself a coonskin cap, to look like Davy Crockett, he was off. Since there were no forks in the road (only an occasional knife dropped by an Indian), he was able to press relentlessly westward, pausing now and then to pose for a bronze statue. As one historian says: "His name is a synonym for pioneering, courage, sagacity, and endurance." To save all these words, therefore, you need only say Boone.

The Salvation Army was established in the United States on March 10, 1880. S.A., which had formerly stood for South America, *Sociedad Anónima*, and sex appeal, took on a new meaning, and the tambourine industry, which had been in the doldrums, was revitalized.

11 On March 11, 1810, Napoleon was married by proxy to Marie Louise, daughter of Emperor Francis I of Austria. He was too busy to attend the wedding, and besides had a horror of getting rice down his neck and having to take off his uniform. Also, his trousers fit so tight that he knew he would be unable to kneel at the altar. But, though he skipped the nuptials, he attended the honeymoon in person.

12 The Blizzard of 1888 struck New York City on March 12 of, by coincidence, 1888. With spring just around the corner, it was considered not only unseasonable but unreasonable, and resentful New Yorkers stood in long lines to get their overcoats back from the cleaner. It was a Great Blizzard, all right, and the more it was talked about, in the years that followed, the greater it became. Few are now alive who can say, every time there is a heavy snowfall, "This is nothing. You should have seen the Blizzard of '88." We must be thankful for small favors.

13 On March 13, 1665, Samuel Pepys wrote in his diary: "This day my wife began to wear light colored locks, quite white almost, which, though it makes her look very pretty, yet, not being natural, vexes me. I will not have her wear them." As is to be expected, later entries in the diary suggest that Mr. Pepys had no success as a home hair stylist or even as a consultant.

Earmuffs were patented by Chester Greenwood of Farmington, Maine (where they were really needed), on March 13, 1877. People who put them on, snugly covering their ears, stopped saying "Br-rr" and said "Whazzat?" instead.

14 On March 14, 1933, Congress authorized the manufacture and sale of 3.2 beer, popularly (but without enthusiasm) called "near beer." The best thing about it was that it came in bottles which could be used for home brew. This was a type of beer that was made in the cellar, during the Prohibition Era, and should not be shaken because (1) there was sediment in the bottom and (2) it might blow up. Sometimes it blew up in the cellar without being touched, but no one was alarmed, thinking it only a bunch of gangsters down there, shooting it out.

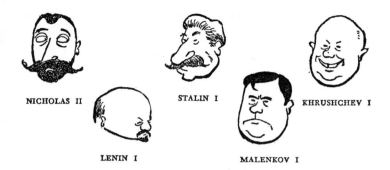

NICHOLAS II

STALIN I

KHRUSHCHEV I

LENIN I

MALENKOV I

15 Czar Nicholas II of Russia abdicated on March 15, 1917. He was the last of the Romanovs, who had ruled Russia for 304 years. After Nicholas II came Lenin I, Stalin I, Malenkov I, and Khrushchev I. Under the Communists, no leader dared to be Second, or even tied for First. Nobody missed the Romanovs, least of all the Bolshevik firing squad.

16 On March 16, 1697, Hannah Dustan was captured by Indians in an attack on Haverhill, Massachusetts. Imprisoned in an Indian camp, Hannah grabbed a tomahawk and slew ten redskins. Were they surprised! In later years, whenever doubt was expressed about her story, she produced the ten scalps, and skeptics were convinced, as well as nauseated. Among the awards she received for her exploit was a pewter tankard from the Governor of Maryland, who thought something manly would be appropriate.

17   Everyone knows that this is St. Patrick's Day, but only Bostonians know that this is also Evacuation Day, the anniversary of the withdrawal of British troops from Boston during the Revolution. Some believe that the British were not driven out of Boston, but desperately wanted an excuse to leave the place. This was before the Old Howard was established, and even the British found the evenings intolerably dull.

On March 17, 1906, speaking before members of the Gridiron Club in Washington, President Theodore Roosevelt coined the word "muckrake." Muckraking seems to have gone out of fashion, not for lack of muck but for lack of muckrakes, as you will discover if you go into a store and try to buy one.

18   This is the birth date, in 1844, of Nikolas Rimsky-Korsakov, the Russian composer. Rimsky-Korsakov is popularly known for "The Flight of the Bumblebee," in which the buzzing of a bee is so successfully imitated that at one point listeners shield their faces with their hands and duck for cover. It may not be great music, but it proves conclusively the fact that a violin can make like a bumblebee more effectively than a bumblebee can make like a violin.

The first electric shaver, invented by Colonel Jacob Schick, went on sale on March 18, 1931. The principle of the electric shaver is that whiskers can be worn down if something is rubbed back and forth across them long enough. The same result, if time is no object, can be obtained by using a nail file, working on whiskers one by one.

The return of the swallows

19 On this date the swallows traditionally return to San Juan Capistrano Mission in California. One swallow may not make a summer, but a whole flock of them flying north on March 19 strongly suggests the approach of spring, or at least of swallows. The custodian at the mission is said to view the return of the birds with mixed feelings.

20 It was on March 20, 1852, that Harriet Beecher Stowe's famous book, *Uncle Tom's Cabin,* was published. It became the first American novel to sell one million copies, no doubt because of the literary style and turn of phrase displayed in such poignant passages as "I 'spect I growed. Don't think nobody never made me" and "I's wicked—I is. I's mighty wicked. . . . I can't help it." (When reading aloud, one should pronounce the last words as "I cain' he'p it." This way one gets the full flavor.

21 This is the first day of spring, when trees become leafy, flowers begin to bloom, and there is a delicate fragrance in the air you could detect if you hadn't a cold.

22 Anthony Van Dyck, the Flemish painter, was born on March 22, 1599. Most of the men in Van Dyck's paintings wear pointed beards, known as Van Dycks. This has led to a certain amount of confusion, because when it is said of someone, "He has a Van Dyck," it is not clear whether he possesses a pointed beard or a valuable painting. There is less chance for misinterpretation when the statement is: "She has a Van Dyck."

23 On March 23, 1775, Patrick Henry made his famous speech, an appeal to arm against England, which contained the ringing challenge: "Give me liberty or give me death!" He did not express a preference, but indicated he would be satisfied with either. The colonies were electrified, which put them a hundred years ahead of the British.

On this day in 1929 President Herbert Hoover had a telephone installed on his desk in the White House. By this revolutionary step he saved precious minutes spent running to and from the corner drugstore.

24 On March 24, 1603, the crowns of England and Scotland were joined, James VI of Scotland becoming James I of England. James, you may be sure, liked the idea of getting a lower number. Besides, with one crown doing the work of two, the spare could be sold to some king with the same head size.

25 On March 25, 1946, the Cuban government reported the theft of a diamond worth nearly $10,000, which had been set into the floor of the national capitol in Havana. Apparently it was meant to pretty up the foyer, or to be a conversation piece. Anyhow, the place where the diamond had been was filled with cement (it took only a little), and the loss went into the federal budget under the heading: Experience.

26 Walt Whitman, the Good Gray Poet, died on March 26, 1892. He was seventy-three, and good and gray. Whitman was a nurse in a hospital during the Civil War, and a disappointment to many a brave Union

A disappointment

soldier who had been away from women for months and was looking forward to something a little more voluptuous. The book of poems for which Whitman is best known is *Leaves of Grass*. It aroused much critical controversy over why, for instance, he did not call it *Blades of Grass* or *Leaves on Trees* or *Whitman's Sampler*. Whitman's most effective poem is "Song of Myself," possibly because of his easy familiarity with the subject.

27 On March 27, 1513, Ponce de León, the Spanish soldier and explorer, landed on the coast of Florida. He was looking for the Fountain of Youth, but was unable to find even a decent hotel. Nevertheless, he kept sampling the water, hopefully, and died cold sober at the age of sixty-one.

28 It was on the fateful day of March 28, 1797, that Nathaniel Briggs of New Hampshire happened on the idea of the washing machine. He thought of it when he saw his wife bending over a washtub and wondered. What he wondered about, and how it finally led to the washing machine, is a long story. Since there was no TV in 1797, Nathaniel's washing machine performed double duty, and he spent his evenings sitting in front of the thing, watching the clothes tumble about, while his wife did the ironing.

29 For the first time in recorded history, on March 29, 1848, Niagara Falls stopped flowing. The stoppage, caused by an ice jam in the river above, was terribly disconcerting to honeymooners, who had come to watch the falls and now stood around looking embarrassed and not knowing what to do. After thirty hours, the falls started falling again, and have been pretty dependable ever since. A lack of confidence has remained, however, and some honeymooners pass up Niagara Falls for the Grand Canyon, which can always be counted on.

30 On March 30, 1858, Hyman L. Lipman, of Philadelphia, patented a pencil equipped with an eraser.
Previously, those who had believed in the perfectability of
the human species were confident that man would eventually stop making mistakes. But Lipman, remembering the
quotation from Pope, "To err is human," felt there would
be a continuing market. As it turned out, the eraser on a
pencil always wears out long before the lead. Some realist
may yet come up with an eraser equipped with a pencil.

On this date in 1867, Secretary of State William H.
Seward signed the treaty with Russia whereby the territory
of Alaska was ceded to the United States for $7,200,000.
The place has more than paid for itself by exporting such
basic commodities as ice cubes and Baked Alaska.

31 This is a big month for purchases. On March 31,
1917, the United States bought the Virgin Islands
from Denmark for $25,000,000. Alaska, though much
larger, had cost less than a third as much, but there was
something about the name of these islands that caused
legislators to throw caution to the winds.

Daylight Saving Time was introduced in the United
States on March 31, 1918. At first people were confused
about whether to set their clocks one hour ahead or one
hour back, and they still are.

APRILIS

THE NAME of this month is thought to come from the Latin *aperire*, "to open," because this is the season when buds, windows, and umbrellas begin to open. During Nero's reign, it was called Neroneus, but as soon as everyone was sure the emperor was dead the name was changed to April. Otherwise Browning would have written:

> Oh, to be in England,
> Now that Neroneus is there.

The birthstone for April is "a girl's best friend," the diamond. The diamond is the hardest of stones. The only thing you can scratch a diamond with is another diamond. The only things harder than diamonds are women who collect them.

1 April 1 is known as April Fools' Day, or All Fools' Day, when it is the custom to play practical jokes on your friends and thereby lose them. In parts of Scotland this is known as "hunting the gowk," a gowk being a cuckoo. In other parts it is known as "hunting the cuckoo," a cuckoo being a gowk. In France the person made a fool of is known as a *poisson d'avril*, and one man's gowk is another man's *poisson*.

2 On April 2, 1917, President Woodrow Wilson appeared before a joint session of Congress and called for a declaration of war against Germany, saying that "The world must be made safe for democracy." Republicans balked until they were persuaded that he had not, as they thought, said that "The world must be made safe for Democrats." This is the sort of misunderstanding that might keep us out of war.

3 On April 3, 1776, Harvard conferred the honorary degree of Doctor of Laws on General George Washington. Subsequently, he was sustained through the hard winter at Valley Forge by the knowledge that he was entitled to be called Dr. Washington. Besides being a general, Washington was a wealthy landowner, and Harvard probably expected a building or a generous gift to the scholarship fund. But the good doctor got so busy with the Revolutionary War that any benefactions he may have contemplated, or even hinted at, completely slipped his mind.

4 Grinling Gibbons was born on April 4, 1648. Grinling, by the way, is not the sort of first name given to every Tom, Dick, and Harry. In case you have forgotten, he was the master woodcarver who carved the choir stalls in St. Paul's Cathedral, London. It is very likely he who thought up the puzzling question: "How much wood would a woodcarver carve if a woodcarver would carve wood?" Mr. Gibbons had a ready smile, and his friends called him "Grin" for short.

On April 4, 1841, exactly one month after his inauguration, President William Henry Harrison died of pneumonia. John Tyler, the Vice President, is said to have been down on his hands and knees shooting marbles with his children when the news reached him. As soon as he knew he was the tenth president of the United States, he got up and began walking around like a Chief Executive.

5 On April 5, 1915, in Havana, Cuba, Jess Willard knocked out Jack Johnson and won the heavyweight boxing championship of the world. The knockout came in the twenty-sixth round, just when the spectators began to think this was going on forever. Jess was a huge cowpuncher from Kansas who gave up punching cows when he found it more lucrative to punch people. Later he lost the championship to Jack Dempsey, even though he had a much longer reach. His reach apparently exceeded his grasp.

6 On April 6, 1909, after trying for twenty-three years, Commander Robert E. Peary reached the North Pole. Except for shinnying up it a few times, and planting an American flag, he found little to do, and left. For this exploit he was promoted to rear admiral. When, years later,

Lt. Commander Richard E. Byrd was made a rear admiral for flying over the South Pole, the Navy's promotion system was firmly established.

Buddies

7 William Wordsworth, the English poet, was born on April 7, 1770. Wordsworth was a great lover of nature, and could sit for hours talking to a daisy or a daffodil. " 'Tis my faith," he said, "that every flower enjoys the air it breathes," and he never plucked a bud, or even pressed the stem of a flower with his thumb and forefinger, for fear of throttling its little windpipe. He was the founder of the SPCF (Society for the Prevention of Cruelty to Flowers), and just couldn't seem to get enough of nature. Not until seventy years after his death was it generally known that this simple nature lover had had a natural daughter by Annette Vallon, a French girl whose woodsy fragrance he apparently admired.

8   Lorenzo de' Medici, the famous Florentine patron of the arts, died on April 8, 1492. Known as Lorenzo the Magnificent, he seems not to have passed along his propensity for good luck to his son and successor, Pietro the Unfortunate. Lorenzo was only forty-three when he died, and his passing cast a pall of gloom over hundreds of sculptors, painters, and architects, who didn't know where their next patron was coming from. His son, Pietro, who couldn't tell a Botticelli from a Spaghetti, ruled Florence for only a couple of years, and then was banished, running from the angry mob in a hail of sticks, stones, and *objets d'art*.

9   On April 9, 1865, the Civil War ended at Appomattox Court House, Virginia, with the surrender of General Robert E. Lee to General Ulysses S. Grant. Lee handed Grant his sword, in token of surrender, and Grant was touched, but fortunately not by the point, else there would have been more bloodshed.

On April 9, 1928, Mae West made her debut in New York in a play entitled *Diamond Lil*. At first glance she seemed to be wearing a life preserver, and one man who was trying to verify this fell out of the first balcony. Critics called the play "shocking," "suggestive," and "in questionable taste," and it settled down for a long run.

10   On this date in 1849, Walter Hunt of New York City startled the world by patenting the safety pin.

Arbor Day

Arbor Day was first observed in Nebraska on April 10, 1872. On this day it is the practice for schoolchildren to plant trees, some of which survive despite being planted upside down. Children are great lovers of trees, delighting in climbing them, building tree houses in them, and pulling down their lower branches to see how far they will bend before breaking. Arbor Day is a reminder to everyone to keep children away from trees.

11 On April 11, 1689, William and Mary were crowned King and Queen of England. There were two thrones, marked "His" and "Hers," two crowns, and two scepters. It was an historic attempt to prove that two can rule as cheaply as one. During their reign, when British subjects sang the national anthem they had to hurry a bit to get in "God save the King and Queen." William, a Dutchman, had formerly been the Prince of Orange, and he thought Mary was a peach. If she had a little fuzz on her cheeks, he didn't mind.

12 The Civil War began on April 12, 1861, when Confederate forces fired on Fort Sumter, a Northern stronghold in Charleston harbor. The cannonading by the Confederates lasted for two days, but there would have been no casualties (some say the Confederates were firing square cannon balls) had not the loyal men of Fort Sumter, after surrendering, fired a salute to the Union flag. This cost one dead and five wounded, and they failed to hit the flag at that.

13 Frank W. Woolworth, originator of the five-and-ten-cent store, was born on April 13, 1852. Being born on the thirteenth was not unlucky for him, for he became immensely wealthy as the money rolled in. (Nickels and dimes rolled very easily.) The purchasing power of a nickel has declined considerably since old F.W.'s day. Anyone who goes into a five-and-ten today had better take five or ten dollars.

On April 13, 1865, General William T. Sherman took Raleigh, North Carolina. This was just after his famous "March to the Sea," which was longer than any of the marches by John Philip Sousa, but not nearly as loud. General Sherman is credited with having coined the expression, "War is hell," though he may have picked it up from one of his foot soldiers, slogging along across Georgia and North Carolina, while General Sherman rode a horse.

14 It was on April 14, 1910, that President William Howard Taft inaugurated an annual custom by throwing out the first ball at the opening of the baseball season. Ever since, the ability to throw a baseball has been one of the basic criteria in choosing a President. It ranks

Running bases

almost with the knack of signing an important document with seventeen pens. Mr. Taft managed to throw the ball far enough that it cleared his stomach, quite a feat in itself, and this brought a roar of applause from the spectators. Many hoped he would take his turn at bat, and get a hit, for they would have loved to see the President running bases. But he had had his athletic activity for the day, and was busy with a Taft-size bag of popcorn.

15 Pierre Rousseau, the French painter, was born on April 15, 1812. Unlike the other Rousseau, Jean Jacques, who believed people should return to nature, Pierre painted landscapes and returned nature to people, framed, and with his signature in the corner. This made it easier for nature lovers who disliked the outdoors. Often in Rousseau's paintings there is a tiger or some other beast peering out through the greenery and signifying something, such as an innate hungering after human flesh.

16 April 16, 1850, marked the death of Madame Marie Tussaud, proprietor of the famous waxworks in London. This is not a place where wax is manufactured, but where there are wax figures of famous personalities. In addition to kings, queens, and presidents, there are such beloved characters as Captain Kidd, Jack the Ripper, and sundry cutthroats, stranglers, and rapists poised for action. Noting the headless figure of a decapitated murderer, one lady visitor is said to have exclaimed, "How lifelike!" Guards pretend to be wax figures also, and when they suddenly move there is a good chance that someone will faint dead away, to the general amusement.

17 On this day in 1704 appeared the first successful newspaper in America, the Boston *News-Letter*. At its peak it reached a circulation of 300. What the publisher needed to increase circulation was something really juicy, like an illicit love affair between the local preacher and one of his parishioners. He seems to have overlooked the Hester Prynne case.

18 Hardly a man is now alive who remembers, without looking it up, that Paul Revere made his famous ride on April 18, 1775. It was midnight when Paul spotted a lantern blinking in Old North Church and rode through the New England countryside, rousing everyone with his cry, "The British are coming!" Undoubtedly there were those who remained dead to the world and others who turned over and went back to sleep, muttering, "Let them come. I've got to get my eight hours." However, Paul did manage to rouse a British patrol, which captured him.

19 On April 19, 1892, Charles E. Duryea of Springfield, Massachusetts, completed the first American-made automobile and went for a drive. Mr. Duryea called his vehicle a "buggyaut," perhaps realizing he did not yet have all the bugs out of it. He had considered calling it a "wrinklemobile" until all the wrinkles were ironed out.

Having been recalled from Korea by President Truman, on April 19, 1951, General Douglas MacArthur closed his military career by addressing a joint session of Congress. This was the famous speech in which he said, "Old soldiers never die; they just fade away." There was not a dry eye in the House, or in the Senate, either. Many were touched to think of the General's fading away into the penury and obscurity of chairman of the board of a large corporation.

20 On April 20, 1902, Marie and Pierre Curie isolated one gram of radium salts from about eight tons of pitchblende. After this, looking for a needle in a haystack was child's play. Marie and Pierre were a man-and-wife team of scientists who worked together harmoniously in the laboratory, she washing the beakers and test tubes and he wiping. They proved that marriage and a career can go hand-in-hand, and that it is fun to experiment together.

21 Rome was founded by Romulus on April 21, 753 B.C. Had his brother thought of the idea, the city would have been called Reme. Romulus and Remus were suckled by a wolf, with whom they had become acquainted. It is a familiar scene, portrayed in numerous paintings and statues, showing R. and R. about to take a drink and trying to choose from a number of spigots. The wolf stands by patiently, like a soda jerk.

22 On April 22, 1864, Congress authorized the Director of the Mint to use the motto "In God We Trust" on coins. The motto was originally proposed by a clergyman, the Reverend M. R. Watkinson. A banker would more likely have suggested a phrase indicating trust in earthly collateral.

23 This is probably the birthday of William Shakespeare, who was born in Stratford-on-Avon in 1564. Francis Bacon was born three years earlier, in 1561, but not on April 23, which is another good reason why he wrote Shakespeare's plays. For those requiring further proof, it should be pointed out that Shakespeare was called the Bard, and the first two letters of Bard and Bacon are identical. As an absolute clincher, listen to this: the last letter in Francis Bacon's first name is the same as the first letter in William Shakespeare's last name!

24 The Library of Congress was established on April 24, 1800, when Congress voted $5,000 for the purchase of books to be used by its members. Now that books were available, Congressmen no longer had to use bricks to hold down the papers on their desks when someone opened a window or made a speech.

25 April 25, 1792, marks the first official use of the guillotine in Paris. Any heads cut off before this time were only to see whether the blade was sharp enough. Before lowering the device, on these occasions, the executioner shouted, "Testing, testing," to reassure the person about to be decapitated. Contrary to popular belief, this revolutionary beheader was not invented by Dr. Joseph I.

Guillotin. He merely recommended the use of some sort of mechanized knife, wishing to introduce a little automation into the onerous business of chopping by hand. Dr. Guillotin was considerate of executioners.

On April 25, 1816, Lord Byron separated from his wife and left England, a social outcast, never to return. He took on various aliases, such as Childe Harold and Don Juan, and wandered restlessly from mistress to mistress. As his poems of this period reveal, he felt terribly sorry for himself. Any young man who is rich, handsome, famous, and surrounded by beautiful women will understand his attitude of melancholy, even despair.

26 On this day in 1607, Captain John Smith landed at Cape Henry, Virginia, to establish a permanent English colony in America. Smith had many hair-raising adventures, including almost having his scalp lifted by Indians, and wrote of them in a work called *A True Relation,* which he apparently expected us to believe. In view of the fact that he spells Chesapeake "Chissiapiacke," we shall always wonder what was the real name of the king of the Pamauncks, whom he refers to as Opeckankenough. Just to be different, we shall make no reference to the fact that Captain John Smith's life was saved by Pocahontas.

27 April 27 was an important day in the career of Ulysses S. Grant. On April 27, 1822, he was born, and, though he died in 1885, it was not until April 27, 1897 that Grant's Tomb was dedicated. This was such an appropriate place for his body, which had been kicking around (or lying around) somewhere else, that it is a wonder no one had thought of it sooner.

28 It was April 28, 1789, when mutiny broke out on the British ship *Bounty*. Captain William ("Bread-fruit") Bligh, who bore a striking resemblance to Charles Laughton, was set adrift in a small boat with eighteen sailors. They rowed more than 3,600 miles to the nearest island, all of them (except the captain, who sat in the stern looking grumpy) becoming experienced oarsmen in the process. Under the command of Fletcher Christian, the mutineers sailed for Tahiti, eager to see whether the women looked the way they did in the travel films. Then most of them went on to Pitcairn Island, where they lived happily for many years, now and then amusing themselves by bashing in a coconut, each time imagining that it was the skull of their old skipper.

29 A significant date in history is April 29, 1913, for on that day the all-purpose zipper was patented by Gideon Sundback of Hoboken, New Jersey. He called it a "separable fastener." What the inventor has been called by people with a stuck zipper and in a hurry cannot be printed in these pages. One thing can be said for the zipper, though. (Bless me, I cannot think what it is!)

30 On April 30, 1900, Casey Jones took his "farewell journey to that promised land" when his Cannonball Express collided with the back end of a freight train on the Illinois Central Railroad near Vaughan, Mississippi. Great as was his impact on the freight train, he made an even greater contribution to barber-shop balladry. People came to know as much about Casey at the Throttle as they did about Casey at the Bat. All of us who are neither singers nor reciters have become a little sick of hearing of both Caseys. Anything can be run into the ground, including a locomotive.

MAIUS

MAY is possibly derived from Maia, an obscure Roman goddess, although it could come from Maius, or "Great," which was one of Jupiter's favorite nicknames. It was regarded as an unlucky month for marriage by the ancient Romans, though some of the more ancient were lucky to get married at all. In medieval England people got up with the dawn and went a-Maying. This consisted of going to the fields and forests and bringing back branches of trees and flowers, a merry custom which forced landowners to put up signs reading "Keepe Offe," "Do Not Picke Ye Bloomers," and "Trespassers Will Be Shotte." Features of May Day include Maypoles (from which comes maypole syrup), Mayonnaise, Mayhap, and Mayhem.

1   On May 1, 1898, Commodore Dewey sailed into
    Manila Bay against the Spanish and uttered the
famous command, "You may fire when you are ready,
Gridley." This is usually taken to indicate that the commodore was calm and unruffled, but he may have been
sarcastic, Gridley being a notorious slowpoke. "Within
five hours," we are told, "the Spanish fleet was reduced to
scrap iron." Once he got going, Gridley was thorough.

2   On May 2, 1865, President Andrew Johnson offered
    a reward of $100,000 for the capture of Jefferson
Davis, President of the Confederacy. The guard around
President Davis was doubled, not to protect him from the
enemy but so that the guards could watch each other. For
$100,000 there is no telling what a man will do. Even Mrs.
Davis had a dreamy look in her eyes.

3   Lord Byron (of whom we are especially fond; see
    entries above) swam the Hellespont on May 3, 1810,
in one hour and ten minutes. He was emulating Leander,
who used to swim across at night to visit Hero, a beautiful
priestess. Hero used to direct Leander's course by holding
up a lighted torch, which made her look for all the world
like the Statue of Liberty. As he waded up the shore,
Leander was wont to cry, "My Hero!" Had Byron had a
beautiful priestess carrying a torch for him, he might have
cut several minutes off his time.

Airplane passenger service was inaugurated on May 3,
1919, when a pilot flew two women from New York City
to Atlantic City, New Jersey. There is no record of complaints having been lodged with the airline, even though
no food was served aboard, there were no magazines, and

the pilot failed to announce the altitude, ground speed, and other matters of interest. Nor do records reveal why the two women didn't take the train for such a short trip.

4 On May 4, 1938, Adolf Hitler and Benito Mussolini met in Rome and pledged "eternal friendship," Rome being the Eternal City. Since the time is not yet up, it is presumed that they still feel that way about each other. Indeed, considering their present locale, their friendship is no doubt warmer than ever.

Maximilian was unsure

5 This is Cinco de Mayo Day in Mexico, celebrating a famous battle in which the outnumbered Mexicans defeated the French, who were trying to put the Archduke Maximilian of Austria on the throne. Maximilian, none too sure of either his claim to the throne or his Spanish, said, "I am the Emperor of Mexico, I cinco." He was laughed out of court, and in court too, for that matter.

6 Two famous men born on this day were Sigmund Freud, in 1856, and Rudolpho Alfonzo Raffaelo Pierre Filibert Guglielmi de Valentina d'Antonguolla, in 1895. Sigmund Freud remained Sigmund Freud, but the other fellow changed his name, at the request of an exasperated motion picture director, to Rudolph Valentino. One likes to think, nonetheless, of Vilma Banky's looking into the eyes of the Great Lover and murmuring, "Kiss me, Filibert."

7 On May 7, 1824, Ludwig van Beethoven's Ninth Symphony was presented for the first time, making possible (if not probable) the following hilarious dialogue:

Spectator at race track, hearing music of band: "Beethoven's Ninth."
Other spectator, binoculars to eyes: "Who's first?"

8 The first dog show of importance was held at the Hippodrome in New York City on May 8, 1877, though there had been a dog show of sorts (and of dogs) at Barnum's American Museum fifteen years earlier. Barnum had employed a barker, whereas in the later show each dog was his own.

9 On May 9, 1907, Miss Anna Jarvis of Philadelphia proposed that the second Sunday of May be set aside as Mother's Day. Since Miss Jarvis, as far as is known, was not a mother at the time, she cannot be accused of self-seeking.

10 On May 10, 1869, Governor Leland Stanford of California drove a golden spike into the last railway tie at Promontory Point, Utah, thereby completing the first transcontinental railway in America. This was followed by a gala celebration, in which there was much drinking of champagne. Whether anyone remained sober enough to sneak back for that gold spike, history does not record, but it is doubtful that anyone prowling around the railway ties at Promontory Point today would have any luck.

11 On May 11, 1832, the first national political platform was adopted at a meeting of (just to show you how mixed up they were) "Democrat-Republican delegates," in Washington, D.C. As a matter of fact, the convention, nominating Henry Clay for President, had been held the previous December. Not being quite sure of the name of his party, and with no platform to stand on for five months, it is no wonder Clay was defeated by Andrew Jackson, a Jacksonian Democrat who stood firmly on his two feet. Political platforms of both parties were taken seriously for several years.

12 On this day in 1919, Henry Ford began a $1,000,000 libel suit against the Chicago *Tribune* for calling him an "anarchist." Mr. Ford felt this was strong language to apply to anyone, even the maker of the Model T, and was fit to be tried. In the end, he won damages of six cents, which he plowed back into the Ford Motor Company. It was Henry Ford who reportedly made the famous remark, "History is bunk!" Ever since, the Ford Foundation has been trying to make amends by giving fellowships and grants to historians.

13 On May 13, 1940, having been named Prime Minister, Winston Churchill rose in the House of Commons and made his well-known and oft misquoted acceptance speech: "I have nothing to offer but blood, toil, tears, and sweat." A politician in the United States would have offered much more, or indicated to his audience that he was just kidding. Few know that this is a paraphrase of a speech by Garibaldi, who declared: "I offer hunger, thirst, forced marches, battles, and death." Garibaldi thus offered more things than Churchill.

14 During World War II, on May 14, 1942, the Women's Army Auxiliary Corps was established by Congress. At first its members were called WAACs, but after a while one A was dropped out as an economy measure. These young women accomplished complicated and hazardous military missions, such as changing a typewriter ribbon while talking over the telephone, and effected important savings in manpower. In fact, the man-hours they saved are said to have been approximately equal to the man-hours lost as a result of distracting soldiers from their duties.

15 This is Straw Hat Day in the United States, when well-dressed men switch from felts. We hear a great deal about the last straw, but this is one day when attention is paid to the first.

16 It was on May 16, 1763, that James Boswell first met Samuel Johnson. The meeting took place in the back parlor of a London bookshop, this being in the days when bookshops were not run by little old ladies and attracted much the same clientele as pubs. Had Boswell talked and Johnson listened, we might have had Johnson's

Johnson did the talking

Life of Boswell, which would have been a lot sexier. But Johnson did the talking, and Boswell had to content himself with being a Great Biographer.

On May 16, 1866, the United States five-cent piece was authorized. This has always been referred to as the "nickel," though it actually consists of 25 per cent nickel and 75 per cent copper, while an occasional coin, known as a "slug," is 100 per cent lead. Vice President Thomas Riley Marshall made the famous statement: "What this country needs is a good five-cent cigar," which led F.P.A. to make the less famous but more significant statement: "What this country needs is a good five-cent nickel."

17 Edward Jenner, the English physician who discovered vaccination, was born on May 17, 1749. The first time he said brusquely to a patient, "Roll up your sleeve," the fellow clenched his fists and assumed a defensive posture, thinking the doc was picking a fight. When he saw Dr. Jenner's needle, he fainted dead away.

18 On this day in 1725, **King George I of England** established the Order of the Bath. There was only one bathroom in the palace, and George was sometimes beaten to it by the Court Chamberlain, the Ladies in Waiting (who could wait only just so long), and the Privy Councilor, a man who thought his title gave him special privileges. The Order of the Bath made it clear that the King came first, then the Queen, and so on.

On May 18, 1910, Halley's comet passed across the sun, and millions of people were confident that the world was coming to an end. But as days passed without anything happening, their confidence was somewhat shaken. Those who had hoped for an excuse to get out of work went off disconsolately to the office or the kitchen sink. Others, who had spent their life's savings in a final spree, could kick themselves. All in all, Halley's comet made quite a mess of things, and Somebody up there was laughing.

19 Anne Boleyn, the second of King Henry VIII's wives, was beheaded on May 19, 1536. The King charged her with adultery, which for a Queen was not cricket. (It was adultery.) The execution took place on Tower Green in London, and was handled with finesse by an expert imported from France. It wasn't everybody who could have an imported executioner, as Henry pointed out to Anne, trying to impress upon her the advantages of being of royal (he spoke the word softly) blood. Anne was the mother of the future Queen Elizabeth, who never married and so never ran the risk of being charged with adultery. Elizabeth cannily beheaded other people instead of being beheaded herself. Unlike her father, she was not the sort to send to France for an executioner, not with all that local talent. After Anne's untimely death, Henry had four more wives, each of whom just lived from day to day.

20 Charles A. Lindbergh started off on what was to be the first solo nonstop airplane flight across the Atlantic on May 20, 1927. Oddly enough, Amelia Earhart Putnam made the first solo plane flight by a woman exactly five years later, on May 20, 1932. Going together seems not to have occurred to them. Lindbergh still could have said he made the first transatlantic flight by a single man, because he was not yet married. Charles flew from New York to Paris, while Amelia flew only from Newfoundland to Ireland, which was like playing a golf course from the women's tees.

21 Alexander Pope, the English poet, was born on May 21, 1688. It was Pope who made the pronouncement, "A little learning is a dangerous thing," which has been a great encouragement to those who prefer to remain ignorant. He also said, "To err is human, to forgive divine," which is often quoted by persons who have made a mistake and hope you will let them off easy. Unless you want the satisfaction of playing God, your best answer is: "To be unforgiving is also human, and that's good enough for me." Pope wrote mostly in couplets, though occasionally in his street clothes. When he was a small boy, he tells us, he lisped in numbers, though apparently not in words, and this annoyed his arithmetic teacher no end.

The first bicycle was seen on the streets of New York on May 21, 1819, having been imported from England. As bicycles increased in number, they became a hazard to pedestrians. Later, as automobiles increased in number, they became a hazard to bicycles, which virtually disappeared from the streets of New York. Thus we have the cycle's cycle.

22 This is National Maritime Day, because on May 22, 1819, the *Savannah*, the first American-made steamship to cross the Atlantic, set forth on its voyage, reaching Liverpool on June 20 with no passengers aboard. Before you get the idea that the passengers had all jumped overboard because of boredom, or overboardom, it might be well to remark that no passengers signed up for the trip in the first place. The members of the crew were getting paid for being out in the middle of the ocean in a vessel in which the steam pressure could cause an explosion any minute, but there was no reason to pay for the privilege, even the minimum off-season rate.

23 On May 23, 1701, Captain William Kidd was hanged in London. For years he had roamed the seas, robbing, murdering, baring chests of hair and burying chests of gold, and becoming a hero to generations of kids (no kin) who played pirate. It was a shame to see him go, and many at the hanging had a lump in their throats, as, in fact, did Captain Kidd.

24 It was on May 24, 1626, that Peter Minuit, of the Dutch West India Trading Company, who had landed May 4, bought the island of Manhattan (or Minuitan) from the Indians. He paid them the equivalent of $24, in beads, according to the current rate of exchange of so many beads to the dollar. This was a mere handful of beads, though we have never been able to learn whether it was a heaping handful or a level handful. At any rate, the Indians were sure they were getting much the better of it. Once the deal was made, Peter Minuit lost no time founding the colony of New Amsterdam and sending home a terse message which read: "This is a large country. Send more beads."

25 On May 25, 1935, Babe Ruth hit his seven hundred fourteenth, and last, home run. It was the End of an Era. Or, as the scoreboard read after the Babe had trotted around the bases, doffing his cap to the cheering crowd in the stands: 1 hit, 1 run, 1 era.

26 On May 26, 1954, the funeral ship of Egyptian King Cheops was unearthed in Egypt. Cheops seems to have gone down with his ship, right in the midst of solid limestone, along with his mummy and other members of the royal family. The inscription on the prow, deciphered after many centuries, reads: "Good-by, Mr. Cheops."

27 Amelia Bloomer, the American feminist and dress reformer, was born on May 27, 1818. It was she who gave her name (her last name, else they would have been called amelias) to bloomers. These may be described, objectively, as "loose trousers gathered in below the knees." Since they never blew up in the wind, or forced a woman to

Amelia Bloomer

take short steps while walking, they obviously had many advantages over skirts, and even more under them. They might be in popular use today but for men.

28 On May 28, 1934, in a farmhouse near Callander, Ontario, Canada, Mrs. Oliva Dionne gave birth to quintuplets. Since her marriage at the age of 16, Mrs. Dionne had had six children, all of them singles. But now, at the age of 25, she let herself go. She and Papa Dionne had always thought birth control meant having one child at a time. On this occasion, as the little ones kept coming out as if they would never stop, they were torn between embarrassment and hope of setting a new record.

29 May 29, 1453, is an important date, since it is when Constantinople, the capital of the Byzantine Empire, was captured by the Turks, and this sort of thing

67

doesn't happen every day. Many historians consider this to be the end of the Middle Ages, though few living at that time realized, when they went to bed, that when they awoke in the morning it would be Modern Times. Else they would surely have stayed up until midnight making the welkin ring and growing misty-eyed for auld lang syne.

30 On May 30, 1883, there was a rumor that the Brooklyn Bridge, which had opened only six days before, was about to collapse. There was such a crush of people around the bridge, waiting for it to fall and growing increasingly impatient, that twelve persons were trampled to death and forty more injured. The moral of this is: Cross your bridges as soon as you come to them; don't stand around gawking.

31 A memorable day is May 31, 1933, when Sally Rand won sudden renown with her fan dance. This took place at Chicago's Century of Progress Exposition, and was apparently meant to show the progress made by women since the time of Queen Victoria, who could do nothing more with a fan than hold it in front of her when she coughed. It was amazing how Sally could make two fans cover so much territory. During her performance, the Hall of Science was practically deserted, even the scientists forsaking their exhibits in order to attend the dance, which they looked at with scientific detachment through binoculars.

JUNIUS

THE ORIGIN of the name of this month is in doubt, which has led scholars to advance their respective theories with more than usual certainty. Some believe it was named June in honor of Juno, but this is obviously too obvious. Others derive it from Junius Brutus, the first consul, which is also child's play. More interesting is the theory that its source is juniores, or young men, in whom the sap starts to rise this time of year.

1 On June 1, 1813, Captain James Lawrence, commander of the *Chesapeake*, uttered the valiant cry, "Don't give up the ship!" as he was carried mortally wounded from his post on deck during an engagement with the British frigate *Shannon*. It would be a pleasure to say that the crew of the *Chesapeake*, stirred by their captain's words, fought on to victory, or to the last man. But it would be untrue. They gave up the ship. When around Navy men, it is just as well not to go into details.

Lizzie Borden, a principal in one of the most sensational murder cases in U.S. history, died at the age of sixty-seven on June 1, 1927. She was charged with murdering her father and stepmother with a sharp weapon, something presumably sturdier than her fingernails, but was acquitted when the murder weapon could not be found. Later, while remodeling the old Borden house in Fall River, Massachusetts, carpenters came upon a rusty hatchet concealed behind a partition. Did the prosecution reopen the case and give Lizzie what was coming to her? No, probably because it was not until 1949 that the hatchet was found, and Lizzie (who preferred to be called Lisbeth) had been dead from natural causes for twenty-two years. Time, as they say, heals all wounds, but in this instance it helped the unwounded Lizzie, not her hacked-up father and stepmother.

2 The first night baseball game was played on June 2, 1883, in Fort Wayne, Indiana. How many balls were lost in the darkness in back of right field is anybody's guess. The score, after seven innings, was 19 to 11, and many of the spectators said the game wasn't worth the candlepower.

3 The Duke of Windsor, formerly King Edward VIII, married Wallis Warfield Simpson on June 3, 1937. The event was described by journalist H. L. Mencken as "the greatest news story since the Resurrection," and it probably sold even more newspapers. Mrs. Simpson failed to become Queen, but she gained such titles as the Duchess of Windsor, One of the Ten Best-dressed Women, and, in and around Buckingham Palace, That Woman.

4 On June 4, 1070, Roquefort cheese was accidentally discovered by an anonymous shepherd (no, his name was not Roquefort) who left his lunch of bread and cheese in a cave for several weeks, and returned to find the moldy cheese delicious—or the delicious cheese moldy, depending on your point of view. After this, he took to forgetting his lunch regularly in order to make what came to be called Roquefort cheese. This ingenious man also learned how to find out when the cheese was ready without walking all the way to the cave. He stood on a small hill about a mile south, closed his eyes, lifted his head, and sniffed.

5 At their national convention in Chicago in 1884, Republicans hoped William Tecumseh Sherman would accept the presidential nomination. But on May 5 he sent them a telegram reading: "If nominated, I will not accept; if elected, I will not serve." It was his way of saying he was not available, and as good a way as any. It was General Sherman who said, in another connection, "War is hell," and he apparently had much the same opinion of politics.

6 On June 6, 1816, ten inches of snow fell in New England, beginning "the year in which there was no summer." It was unpleasant, but it provided a sure topic of conversation. Ever since, New Englanders have vainly looked forward to a similar fluke, a year in which there was no winter.

7 George Bryan Brummell, the man who set the fashion in men's clothes in England, was born on June 7, 1778. As Beau Brummel (having suffered the loss of one "l"), he gave his name to the dictionary. Unlike quisling, he was upper class, and therefore remained upper case.

Beau Brummel

Almost anyone would prefer being called a Beau Brummel to being called a fop, though there is no need to be referred to as either if you wear second-hand clothing with frayed cuffs.

8 On June 8, 1869, Ives W. McGaffey of Chicago gave us the vacuum cleaner. In order to make it clear that he was not planning to clean vacuums, he called it a "sweeping machine." Its chief feature, which has been retained through many models, is its peculiar noise. This causes the user to shout, "I can't hear a word you're saying; wait till I turn this thing off," although obviously hearing enough to know you are saying something. Meanwhile you, as you are standing alongside, hear quite distinctly and are sure the operator of the vacuum cleaner is just being perverse.

9 Peter the Great of Russia was born on June 9, 1672. Since he was the first Peter, he could be called Peter the Great without invidious comparisons. However, subsequent Russian rulers with this name could call themselves Peter the Greater and Peter the Greatest, which apparently had not occurred to him. Peter the Great is known for having brought Western civilization to Russia, which will clear up something for people in Europe and America who wonder where Western civilization has gone.

10 On June 10, 1776, the Continental Congress appointed a committee to draft the Declaration of Independence, and anyone who has ever seen a committee at work will wonder how it ever got drafted. Fortunately, Thomas Jefferson was on the committee, and the others were smart enough to hand him a piece of paper and a quill pen and say, "Jot something down, Tom. We will go along."

11 On that memorable day, June 11, 1939, the King and Queen of England tasted their first hot dogs at a picnic given by President and Mrs. Franklin D. Roosevelt at Hyde Park, New York. Reporters and photographers pressed close to get the King's reactions on this historic occasion, compared by some to King John's granting the Magna Carta at Runnymede in 1215. There was a breathless silence (happily, since several of the party had taken their hot dogs with onions), and then His Majesty was seen to clutch his stomach and open his mouth. Was he going to say something or did he have other plans? Proving himself every inch (including his digestive tract) a king, and with a gallantry reminiscent of Sir Walter Raleigh and of Admiral Nelson at Trafalgar, he turned to Mrs. Roosevelt and said, in a loud if slightly quavering voice, "Delicious." Anglo-American relations were further improved when President Roosevelt promised to come to England and eat kippers.

12 Harry Houdini, the great magician, on June 12, 1923, thrilled a large audience in New York by struggling free from a strait jacket, head downward, forty feet above the ground. A few skeptics thought it was a trick. Others marvelled less at his getting out of the strait jacket than at his not, immediately thereafter, falling smack on his head, as did those who went home and tried it.

13 On June 13, 1789, Mrs. Alexander Hamilton gave a dinner party for General George Washington and surprised and delighted her guests by serving ice cream for dessert. George, who could always be counted on for an embarrassing remark, looked earnestly at his hostess and asked, "Did you make it yourself?" "No, General," Mrs. Hamilton replied, stiffening her upper lip, on which there was a bit of cake frosting, "I cannot tell a lie. The whole meal was handled by a catering firm."

14 On June 14, 1898, American troops bound for Cuba and the Spanish-American War sang "There'll Be a Hot Time in the Old Town Tonight." Whether they were thinking of burning Havana or going to a night club in the old part of town, without air-conditioning, we shall never know.

15 In Philadelphia, on June 15, 1752, at the height of a storm, Benjamin Franklin went out to fly a kite. People had always thought Ben a bit odd, and now they looked at each other and smiled. Paying no attention to them, Franklin splashed through puddles as he kept his eyes on an iron key that swung aloft. He was trying to prove that lightning and electricity are related (second cousins once removed or something), and did. He was so happy about the whole thing that he would have stayed out there all day, drenched to the skin, but he had to pull the kite down to retrieve the key, someone wanting to get into his printing shop.

16 Father's Day, observed nationally as the third Sunday in June, first fell on June 16, 1946, though it had been observed in various localities as early as 1910. While the rose is generally recognized as the official flower for the day, there is merit in the idea of the Martin W. Callener Bible Class of Wilkinsburg, Pennsylvania, which

Father's Day

in 1924 selected the dandelion because "the more it is trampled on the more it grows." The symbolism is appropriate enough, but there is surely a point after which the trampling, though stimulating at first, is not conducive to growth, even in a dandelion.

17 On June 17, 1775, American patriots, outnumbered more than three to one, were attacked by the British in the Battle of Bunker Hill. The colonials were prepared, however, since every movement of the British was reported by a lookout in the top of Bunker Hill Monument. The Americans might have won the battle but for the ill-advised order: "Don't fire until you see the whites of their eyes!" They held their fire too long, and were overrun. It seems that the British soldiers had been up late in Boston the night before, looking for fun but unable to find it, and their eyes were bloodshot. By the way, the battle was actually fought not at Bunker Hill but at Breed's Hill, but there is no use changing all the history books now.

18 "Millions for defense, but not one cent for tribute" was the toast proposed by Robert Goodloe Harper at a dinner honoring John Marshall in Philadelphia on June 18, 1798. Charles C. Pinckney, our American minister to France, said practically the same thing a year or two earlier, in Paris, and if he fails to get credit it may be because he said "not a damned penny," which for a long time was not the sort of thing you could quote when ladies were present. At any rate, when it came to tribute both men, though otherwise generous, were penny-pinchers.

19 A vast throng of New Yorkers lined the streets on June 19, 1945, to see General Dwight D. Eisenhower, just returned from victory in Europe. Having lined the streets, they were told by the police to stand behind the lines and stop shoving. Mayor La Guardia gave the general a medal, instead of the traditional key to the city, thinking it more military and having had some complaints, the last time, about the key being too big for most locks around town.

20 At six o'clock on the morning of June 20, 1837, the Archbishop of Canterbury got Princess Victoria of Kent out of bed to tell her that her uncle, King William IV, was dead and that she was Queen of England. Victoria, now eighteen, had until this time shared a room with her mother, the Duchess of Kent, and the first question she asked of the archbishop was, "Will I have a room of my own?" He assured her that she would not only have a room all to herself but her personal throne, which she need not share with her mother unless she became lonesome. This was the beginning of the Victorian Era, when most women followed the Queen's example and slept alone.

21 Prohibition enforcement officers were authorized by Sir Francis Wyatt, the Governor of Virginia, on June 21, 1622. Their job was to report persons who were "disordered," which was the seventeenth-century equivalent of "fried," "stoned," or "blotto." What happened to a disordered person after he was reported, our source does not say. Perhaps he was just left on the police blotter until he dried out.

22 On June 22, 1874, Dr. Andrew Taylor Still, of Macon, Missouri, the founder of osteopathy, cured a case of flux. A case of flux was serious, or at least more so than a single bottle. An osteopath is a doctor who works his fingers to your bone, and to be fully qualified must undergo years of training, including courses in embryology, neurology, anatomy, and finger flexing.

King George of England and his consort, Queen Mary, were crowned in Westminster Abbey on June 22, 1911. A consort can be either a husband or a wife, depending on his or her sex, and is not to be confused with a musical performance.

23 The Secret Service was created by an Act of Congress on June 23, 1860. Its motto was the shortest of any government agency: "Sh!"

24 On June 24, 1440, give or take a few days (and years), Johann Gutenberg invented movable printing types. He did not start printing, though, until about 1450, up to this time getting such a kick out of just moving the type from this place to that. He was helped financially by Johann Fust, a South German who, though he came later than Gutenberg, liked to drawl, "But ah'm still Fust."

25 Governor John Winthrop on June 25, 1630, introduced the table fork to America. He brought it to Massachusetts from England, carrying it in a leather case and being so mysterious about it that he had everyone guessing. Was it a pistol? A camera? A tape recorder? At the first large banquet, he laid the case alongside his plate, and then dramatically opened it, right after the soup course. Indians, looking in through the windows, thought the governor was repeatedly stabbing himself, and expected to see him slump to the floor any minute. When he did not, they revised their opinion and assumed him to be a sword swallower.

George Armstrong Custer

Sitting Bull

Custer's Last Stand took place on June 25, 1876, at the Battle of Little Big Horn, in Montana. On this occasion General George Armstrong Custer stood up just once too often and was creased by a passing tomahawk. He should have learned from his adversary, Sitting Bull, the Sioux Indian chief, who squatted patiently behind a rock until the fracas was over. "Always keepum head down," was S.B.'s priceless advice to young warriors, as they performed a tonsorectomy on Custer.

26 On June 26, 1284, the Pied Piper of Hamelin, Germany, led all the town's children off to Oblivion. Thus he got revenge on the town fathers, who had refused to pay him his fee for clearing the rats out of the ratskeller. The town fathers wished they had paid up, especially when they heard from the town mothers. "Pied," by the way, refers to the parti-colored clothes of the Piper, who probably was all dressed up for a parti.

27 The New York Curb Exchange, where for years it had been possible to exchange curbs that were not exactly the right size or shape, on June 27, 1921, moved indoors, into its own building. Inside, business was carried on as usual, and better than usual during rainy weather. Traders could be observed selling short, when they needed something a little longer, or just sitting around looking worried.

On June 27, 1945, Premier Joseph Stalin, a self-made man, promoted himself to generalissimo.

28 It was on June 28, 1778, in the Battle of Monmouth, that Molly Pitcher heroically took over her mortally wounded husband's cannon. (So it says in one of my sources, though another states that he merely suffered a sunstroke and later returned to duty. This shows how confusing it is to read more than one history book.) Anyhow, Molly Pitcher's real name was Mary Ludwig Hays, and she got the name Pitcher from either (1) the container in which she brought water to the thirsty artillerymen or (2) the way she tossed cannon balls up to them in the heat of battle. For her exploit in taking over her husband's cannon she was made a sergeant, jumping over half a dozen corporals, who looked up with amazement.

29 Peter Paul Rubens, the Flemish painter, was born on June 29, 1577. Early in his career, when he was young and gullible, someone sold him an oversupply of flesh-colored paint, and for years he madly daubed at pictures containing large expanses of nude fat women in order to use it up. Despite the acres and acres of bosoms and buttocks he splashed over canvases, there were still several cans of the paint left at the time of his death. In a museum, you can always tell which is the Rubens Room. It is the one full of stout ladies who, as they look at the pictures, feel almost fragile and sylphlike by comparison. Also among the observers are likely to be a few skinny old men who may not know art but know what they like.

Know what they like

30 On June 30, 1859, crowds gathered to watch Charles Blondin, a French acrobat, walk across Niagara Falls on a tightrope. One false step and —. But every step was true. Though Blondin crossed the falls in five minutes, which was quicker than going around, there was no rush to follow in his footsteps. Most of the spectators seemed willing to wait until a bridge was built. They wanted to see what July was like.

JULIUS

THIS was originally the fifth month, instead of the seventh, and Romulus is said to have named it Quintilis. The name was changed to July in honor of Julius Caesar, who was born in this month. Not everyone can have the month in which he was born named after him, unless we have a great many more months, or fewer first names. The Anglo-Saxons called it Hegmonath, or "haymonth," it being the time of year when those early Englishmen, who were much more gregarious than they are now, went around yelling "Heg!" or "Hay!" at people to get their attention.

1 On July 1, 1898, Lt. Colonel Theodore Roosevelt and his Rough Riders made their victorious assault on San Juan Hill in the Spanish-American War. What routed the Spanish was the way Teddy flashed his teeth at them. With his mustached upper lip clamped tightly down, he rode up within a few yards of the enemy lines and then suddenly let them have one blinding flash.

2 It was on July 2, 1890, that Congress passed the Sherman Act. This is often referred to as the Anti-Trust Act by large corporations that think the government doesn't trust them. (They are right.) But the government seemed to trust the Indians, with whom by this time peace treaties had been concluded, and the practice of scalping was taken over by persons who bought up theater tickets. The Indians were given a few patches of remote, barren land on which it was difficult to grow anything, probably because of all that oil right under the surface.

3 This is when the dog days begin. For about six weeks the weather is hot and humid, and people who haven't done anything go around saying, "I'm dog tired." Others say, "I've been working like a dog," which means lying in the shade asleep.

The first civilian passenger automobile made since the beginning of World War II rolled off the assembly line in Detroit on July 3, 1945. For a few months, automobile salesmen could afford to be haughty and insulting, while prospective buyers prostrated themselves, one of them even crying out, "Run over me, I want to feel that new tread." Then things returned to normal. Customers walked into the showroom to get the salesman's hopes up, and then left after kicking the tires, slamming the doors, and scratching the finish to see whether it would scratch.

4 "America," or "My Country 'Tis of Thee," was first sung in public by Boston school children on July 4, 1832. The words were written by Samuel Francis Smith, a student at Andover Theological Seminary. According to Oliver Wendell Holmes, "Smith's name will be remembered by every school child in the land, when I have been forgotten for a hundred years." Since it is not yet a hundred years since Oliver Wendell Holmes was forgotten, we cannot be sure of the accuracy of this statement.

July 4 is also known as the Fourth of July.

5 This is the birthdate, in 1709, of Étienne de Silhouette, Minister of Finance under Louis XV. This Frenchman gave his name to the well-known form of drawing, perhaps because Louis spent so much on Pompadour and du Barry that his Minister of Finance looked drawn, if not overdrawn.

6 John Paul Jones, who was to become a famous American naval hero, was born in Scotland on July 6, 1747. He was originally John Paul, but got so tired of being asked what his last name was that he added the Jones. Before he entered the American Navy, in 1775, he was a slave trader and a smuggler. What caused him to go straight once he joined the Navy may have been his conscience, or then again it may have been his compass.

In Paris on July 6, 1885, Louis Pasteur inoculated the first human being, a boy who had been bitten by a dog. Previously he had inoculated only dogs that had been bitten by boys.

7 Hawaii was annexed to the United States by approval of a Congressional resolution on July 7, 1898, with formal annexation on August 12. An interesting fact about the Hawaian language is that its alphabet is missing a number of letters, including the *r*, which means that oysters are never in season. Also, the word "aloha" means both "hello" and "good-by," and this causes no end of confusion, since it is impossible to tell whether someone is coming or going. In 1898, so few tourists were lying on the beach at Waikiki that you could still see the sand.

8 On July 8, 1889, in Richburg, Mississippi, John L. Sullivan fought his last bare-knuckle heavyweight championship bout. He defeated Jake Kilrain in the seventy-fifth round. The spectators, who had been sitting on the edge of their seats all this time, were permanently scarred.

July 8 is also the birthdate, in 1839, of John D. Rockefeller, a philanthropist who cautiously gave away his vast wealth a dime at a time. When asked for money, he would sometimes say, "Can you break a quarter?" The Rockefeller Foundation is not, as might be supposed, an undergarment.

Gave away dimes

9   At six o'clock in the evening on July 9, 1776, General George Washington summoned his soldiers and had the Declaration of Independence read to them. The moment the reading was finished, the soldiers threw their hats into the air. This was followed by a scene of indescribable excitement and confusion, during which it was fortunate the British did not attack, when each soldier tried to recover his own hat, or at least one of the same head size.

10   On July 10, 1908, William Jennings Bryan was nominated as the Democratic presidential candidate. He was not nearly so excited about it as he had been the first two times. Nor did Bryan, who took no stock in evolution, think his chances would gradually improve.

The highest temperature ever recorded in the United States was 134 degrees in Death Valley, California, on July 10, 1913. However, this is two degrees short of the world record of 136 degrees established at Azizia, Tripolitania, on September 13, 1922. It is said that a playful native gave a tourist a hotfoot, about midday, and he didn't even notice.

11   On July 11, 1804, Aaron Burr, the Vice President of the United States, and his rival, Alexander Hamilton, fought a pistol duel at ten paces. Hamilton, a slow walker, was mortally wounded. Burr wasn't scratched; in fact, he wasn't even sorry. Why Burr didn't shoot Thomas Jefferson, the President, and thereby gain an immediate promotion, will never be known. At any rate, Jefferson must have felt mighty uncomfortable the rest of his term, having to walk in front of Burr at ceremonials. Every time Burr reached for his handkerchief, Jefferson ducked.

12 Julius Caesar was born on July 12, 100 (or 102) B.C., which will surprise those who thought B.C. stood for Before Caesar. His full name was Gaius (or Caius) Julius Caesar, but after experimenting with various combinations, such as G. J. Caesar, he decided upon simply Julius until such time as he could be called Mighty Caesar or (one he especially liked) O. Mighty Caesar. A person of great energy and diverse talents, he went into many fields, being a general, statesman, orator, poet, historian, and middle-aged lover. What fields he went into with Cleopatra, and how long he stayed, we do not know.

13 On July 13, 1865, in an editorial in the *New York Tribune*, Horace Greeley advised young men on low salaries in government jobs in Washington to go west. But in 1872 Greeley himself became interested in a government job in Washington when he was the Liberal Republican and Democratic candidate for President. (His running mate, you no doubt remember, was B. Gratz Brown.) It is true that Greeley traveled in the West, on one occasion interviewing Brigham Young, who had fifteen wives and told him some things he was unable to print in the *Tribune*. Although Greeley, Colorado, is named after him, he said privately, "The West is a nice place to visit, but I wouldn't want to live there." Most of his life he spent in New York City, giving advice.

14 This is Bastille Day, which is the Fourth of July of France because of the time difference. It celebrates the storming of the Bastille on July 14, 1789, when all the prisoners were let out except a few timid souls who thought it looked safer inside.

15 And here it is St. Swithin's Day, on which, if it rains, there will be forty more days of rain; but if it does not rain, there will be no rain for forty days. Such, at least, is the legend. The weather man uses more scientific methods, such as taking an opinion poll, reading tea leaves, and asking his wife. He also has the good sense not to forecast forty days in advance, preferring such relatively safe pronouncements as "Today it is raining." Swithin was a bishop of Winchester, England, who died in 862, and what he had to do with the weather remains cloudy.

The most important fact about July 15, 1906, to the author, is that he was born.

16 The District of Columbia was established by Congress on July 16, 1790, with Washington as the permanent capital of the United States. The city is now full of monuments, a tribute to the great men of our history and to the Vermont marble lobby. It is also full of the relatives of officeholders, who are willing to sharpen pencils and empty wastebaskets as long as they are paid roughly the same salary as an ambassador. Such self-sacrifice must be attributed to patriotism, family ties, and greed.

17 On July 17, 1821, the treaty was ratified, whereby Florida was ceded by Spain to the United States. Spain had no need for it, because her people had a natural tan. In time it came to afford estates for gangsters, winter training camps for baseball teams, homes for retired persons, and occupation for thousands of real estate salesmen, as well as an interesting jog in outline maps of the United States.

In England, on July 17, 1917, King George V issued a proclamation changing the name of the British royal house from Saxe-Coburg-Gotha to Windsor. This dealt a massive blow to the Kaiser, and no doubt speeded the end of World War I.

18 On July 18, 64 A.D., Rome burned. Nero, as everyone knows, fiddled. But the popular notion that he was unconcerned about the conflagration is wrong. To do

Nero fiddling

justice to the poor fellow, he was scraping away for dear life in the hope of attracting attention and summoning the fire department, not knowing how to blow a bugle.

19 Along about now comes the National Cherry Festival held since 1928 at cherry-picking time in Traverse City, Michigan. Everyone enjoys the festivities except a few, with their cheeks bulging and a troubled expression on their faces, who go around mumbling, "Where do you put the pits?"

20 Francesco Petrarca (Petrarch) was born in Arezzo, Italy, on July 20, 1304. This great poet is the author of the beautiful and oft-quoted "Petrarchan Sonnet," which goes:

> Ay bee bee ay,
> Ay bee bee ay,
> See dee, see dee,
> See dee.

He is also credited with having begun the Renaissance in Italy, watching with not a little amazement as it spread unchecked through France and into England. Many of his most passionate love poems were inspired by Laura, the wife of a nobleman, Count Hugues de Sade, by whom she bore eleven children while Petrarch was writing his heart out.

On July 20, 1917, Secretary of War Newton D. Baker drew the first draft number, 258, from a glass bowl containing 10,500 serial numbers. "Will the lucky holder of number 258 please step forward?" asked the Secretary. They collared the man two blocks south of the Senate Office Building, running toward Mexico.

21 The first strike in which the militia was called to keep the peace occurred on July 21, 1828, at Paterson, New Jersey. Workers were hopping mad because the dinner hour in factories had been changed from twelve to one. By one, they were starved, and what with the noise of machinery and their stomachs rumbling, couldn't hear a word anyone said. The ruckus of 1828 ultimately led to significant changes in labor-management relations, the dinner pail becoming the lunch pail and the noon hour taking ninety minutes, preceded by a coffee break.

22 The second "Lost Colony" was established on Roanoke Island, off the coast of what is now North Carolina, on July 22, 1587. The first settlement, consisting of English colonists who came to Roanoke Island in 1585, had disappeared by the time the second group arrived. These in turn had disappeared when a third expedition arrived a few years later. What could the trouble be? Tidal waves? Quicksand? Wrong island? It was pretty discouraging to a colonial power like England, which was beginning to lose face, as well as colonies.

Invention of ice cream cone

23 On this never-to-be-forgotten day in 1904 the ice cream cone was invented by Charles E. Menches of St. Louis, Missouri. Almost immediately there was an upsurge in the business of dry cleaners and manufacturers of cleaning fluid.

24 The Doctor of Music degree was first conferred July 24, 1849, by Georgetown University, and a little research will tell you whom it was conferred upon and anything else you want to know about this fascinating fact. All we wish to point out is that whether you call for an M.D. or a Mus. D. depends on whether you are having trouble with a clavicle or a clavichord.

25 The carrousel, or merry-go-round, was patented by Willhelm Schneider, of Davenport, Iowa, on July 25, 1871. It should be noted that the word "carrousel" is derived from the Italian *carosello*, and has no connection with "carouse," no matter how devilish some riders may feel. One thing Schneider failed to anticipate was the difficulty of persuading a small child to get off after only three or four rides. Many parents look forward to the day when carrousels will be equipped with ejection seats, purchased from Air Force surplus, and children will be picked up at the far end of the Fun Zone.

26 The first airplane wedding took place in the air over Sheepshead Bay Speedway, New York City, on July 26, 1919. Interestingly enough, the bride and groom were in one plane and the minister and best man in another, and it would have lent further excitement had the two planes collided. The bride was given away on the ground by her father, who had a tendency to airsickness and balked at hiring a third plane, anyhow. Quite a crowd gathered beneath the planes, and the bridesmaid who caught the bride's bouquet required eight stitches.

27 Gertrude Stein, the poet, died in Paris on July 27, 1946, at the age of seventy-two. She is best known for her lovely "A rose is a rose is a rose," the idea for which she got from a stuck phonograph needle. She is also remembered for the hauntingly beautiful poem:

> Pigeons on the grass,
> Alas.

This latter inspired an unknown but talented poet to the equally brilliant threnody:

> Pigeons o'er my hat,
> Splat!

28 Whether or not it still exists, there was once a union of women shoemakers, called the Daughters of St. Crispin, and it held its first convention at Lynn, Massachusetts, on July 28, 1869. Their motto, on this historic occasion, was "The last shall be first." Women shoemakers have gradually died out, probably because of their refusal to make anything larger than a 4AAA. "If the shoe fits," they declared, "it is too large."

29 In Puyallup, Washington, the Days of Ezra Meeker begin on July 29 and continue through August 3. These festivities honor that outstanding pioneer, Ezra Meeker, who traveled the Old Oregon Trail by prairie schooner in 1851 and before he died, at the age of ninety-eight, became known as "The Hop King of the World." Ezra, we regret to say, was a grower of hops and not a world champion broad jumper.

30 In the *Cincinnati Gazette* of July 30, 1862, during the Civil War, the term "Copperhead" was first used to designate a Northerner sympathetic to the Southern cause. Since a copperhead is also a venomous snake, this was probably not meant as a compliment. Have you ever wondered what Southerners called a Southerner sympathetic to the Northern cause?

Few will recall that the WAVES, founded on July 30, 1942, got their name from "Women Appointed for Voluntary Emergency Service" in the U.S. Navy. Whatever they did, they did voluntarily, and they threw themselves completely into everything, especially their uniforms when they had overslept. They had to cope with many difficulties, such as keeping the lint off their blues, which they did with considerable pluck. The chief emergency they helped meet during World War II was a lack of women.

31 On July 31, 1947, the Smugglers' Union in Hendaye, France, went on strike because customs guards were permitting French citizens to cross into Spain to buy fruit and wine. Smugglers picketed the French border, carrying signs reading "Frenchmen Go Home: We Deliver," "Think of Our Wives, Mistresses, and Children," and "We Can Get It for You Wholesale." Smuggling survived the crisis, and as a pleasant and profitable activity in France ranks second only to snuggling.

AUGUSTUS

Aᴜɢᴜsᴛ *was named to honor the Emperor Augustus, who in this month had put down a civil war, subdued Egypt, and entered the consulate, which was not just a matter of opening a door. Twelve months like this and he could say, without boasting, that he had had a good year. For those interested in genealogy, Augustus was a grandson of Julius Caesar's sister. He was a dignified, austere type, whom people rarely called Gus. July, as we have seen, was named after Julius Caesar and had thirty-one days. To avoid invidious comparisons, August was made equal in length by taking a day from September, which, not being named after an emperor, was vulnerable.*

1 San Francisco's picturesque cable cars went into operation on August 1, 1873. At first they were known only as cable cars, but the name was soon changed to picturesque cable cars, and since then has never varied, except when, for the sake of alliteration, they are called colorful cable cars.

2 Street letter boxes, for depositing mail, were in use in Belgium as early as 1848, but it was not until August 2, 1858, that such devices were set up in New York and Boston. Since then, countless citizens have searched vainly to find the letter slot in a fire alarm box.

3 The immigration head tax on people coming into the United States was begun on August 3, 1882. Immigrants were charged at a rate of fifty cents a head at that time, though the cost has steadily gone up. We have never been able to get through all the fine print to discover whether shrunken heads may be brought in for proportionately less. At any rate, this will explain the grim tone with which customs inspectors say, "Open that hat box."

4 Percy Bysshe Shelley, the English poet, was born on August 4, 1792. He was a Romantic, which explains why he deserted his wife and ran off with another woman whose intellect he admired. Though Shelley and his first wife were incompatible, they shared a common end: they both drowned. Shelley's second wife was the author of

The Shelleys

Frankenstein, which gives some idea of their married life. "Poetry," Shelley once wrote, "is the record of the best and happiest moments of the happiest and best minds." An example is this line from his "Ode to the West Wind":

> I fall upon the thorns of life! I bleed!

Despite this accident, he lived to the comparatively ripe old age (for a Romantic) of thirty.

5 Flogging was abolished in the United States Army on August 5, 1861. Discipline sagged, and there was little fun left in being an officer. Large supplies of whips, lashes, scourges, and knouts were sold as Army surplus or shipped to needy nations by the Red Cross. Soon it became necessary to issue service stripes, it no longer being possible to indicate length of service by a display of welts. The old order ("Remove shirt and clench teeth") changeth.

6 On August 6, 1832, Johann Kaspar Spurzheim, the famous phrenologist, visited the United States on a lecture tour. By feeling the bumps on anyone's head, he could tell whether the person was talented, likely to succeed, or had been in an accident recently. As Professor Spurzheim went from city to city, feeling heads, he caused an upsurge of interest in phrenology and a dangerous epidemic of dandruff.

7 The revolving door was patented by Theophilus Van Kannel of Philadelphia, on August 7, 1888. It was useful in the winter, letting in only a little cold air at a time, and was generally accepted once people learned not to make a complete circle and come out where they went in. Now and then two people squeezed into the same section and, before extricating themselves, had quite a go around. Before our reserves of coal and oil are depleted, science will no doubt find a way to harness the power generated by the tens of thousands of revolving doors across the nation.

8 Lawn tennis matches for the Davis Cup were first played on August 8–10, 1900, in Boston. The United States soundly defeated England, winning every match, and no wonder. The English team, misled by the fact that they were to play at the Longwood Cricket Club, had brought bats instead of rackets. They were also slowed down by their shin guards.

By declaring war on Japan on August 8, 1945, seven days before Japan's surrender, the Soviet Union snatched victory from the jaws of victory.

9 Jonas Bronck, after whom the Bronx, New York, is named, emigrated from the Old World on August 9, 1638. He bought the Bronx from the Indians, in 1639, for "two guns, two kettles, two coats, two adzes, two shirts, one barrel of cider, and six bits of money," which sounds as though it just about cleaned him out. He also gave his name to the Bronx (or Bronck's) Cheer, a raucous sound he discovered he could make by sticking out his tongue and blowing until it vibrated. Previously he had merely stuck out his tongue without blowing, like everyone else. Bronck was a man you could count on for something a little extra.

10 On August 10, 1776, a committee comprised of Benjamin Franklin, John Adams, and Thomas Jefferson proposed "E Pluribus Unum" as the motto for the Great Seal of the United States. They had run across it in a book of Foreign Words and Phrases, and rather liked the sound as well as the impression it would give that all the Founding Fathers had classical educations. Little did they realize how many persons, a couple of hundred years later, would think E. Pluribus Unum also one of the Founding Fathers, a man whose name was simply Elmer P. Unum until he entered politics and put on airs.

11 On August 11, 1928, accepting the Republican nomination for President, Herbert Hoover stated: "We in America today are nearer the final triumph over poverty than ever before in the history of any land." After the stock market crash of 1929 and the ensuing Depression, there were those who felt Mr. Hoover must have been misquoted, the phrase "the final triumph over" having crept in through careless reporting.

12 Abbott Handerson Thayer, the American painter who discovered camouflage, was born on August 12, 1849. He knew he had discovered something important when a painting on which he was at work disappeared before his very eyes. He might never have found it but for the legs of the easel, from which he triangulated his position. Once he learned to paint this same design on himself, and became invisible, he became famous. He also had some interesting experiences.

13 On August 13, 1923, "Yes, We Have No Bananas" was the number one hit song. Half a million copies of the sheet music were sold in the first three months. What we have always wondered is what it did to the sale of bananas.

14 An International Congress of Esperantists, the first to be held in the United States, met in Washington, D.C., August 14 to 20, 1910. Delegates came from 35 nations, all of them jabbering away in Esperanto, the universal language. However, the first delegate to go into a restaurant and order three-minute eggs, buttered toast, and a cup of coffee, in his best Esperanto, got the following response in English: "Huh?"

15 On August 15, 1943, the War Department awarded the Legion of Merit to Sergeant Edward M. Dzuba for "originating many unusual and appetizing recipes for the utility of leftover scraps." Sergeant Dzuba, who belonged to a medical battalion, felt safe in experimenting, with a stomach pump always close at hand. Nonetheless, the War Department decided against making any reference to the sergeant's good work on recruiting posters.

16 The first international migratory bird legislation was the Migratory Bird Treaty between the United States and Great Britain, signed on August 16, 1916. This permitted birds to fly back and forth across the Canadian border without passports, in fact without even having to open their beaks for customs inspection. It was a fine example of international cooperation, and much appreciated by the birds. Canadian birds could now spend the winter in Florida, while American birds could spend the summer in the Canadian Rockies. Only birds and millionaires can afford this sort of luxury.

17 If the heat bothers you, it may be refreshing to recall that on August 17, 1958, a record low of 124 degrees below zero was recorded in Antarctica, about 400 miles from the South Pole. This, by the way, is considerably lower than the North American record of 81 below, recorded in February, 1947, at an airport in the Yukon called Snag. The person who named the place had a gift for the *mot juste*.

18 Virginia Dare saw the light of day on Roanoke Island, North Carolina, on August 18, 1587. She was "the first child born of English parents on American soil," either because Mrs. Dare owned no bed or was unable to rush back from the fields in time. The first child born of non-English European parents on American soil (but things were much more primitive in those days) was Snorro, a distant relative of Leif Ericson, whose parents settled in Vinland in the year 1007. Unlike Virginia Dare, who had a wine named after her, Snorro has not yet been memorialized by a drink or device, but it could happen any day now.

Concealed her sex

19 Aboard the U.S. frigate *Constitution* (*Old Ironsides*) during its victorious battle with the British frigate *Guerrière*, on August 19, 1812, was a woman named Lucy Brewer. "Concealing her sex," we are told, "she enlisted under the name of George Baker." How Lucy concealed her sex during the medical examination remains a secret. In the rush of war, the young doctor was probably just out of medical school, and inexperienced.

20 Paying tribute to the Royal Air Force, Prime Minister Winston Churchill on August 20, 1940, made his famous statement to the House of Commons: "Never was so much owed by so many to so few." (Apparently he forgot about economic conditions back in feudal times, and the ratio of serfs to lords.) One source gives not August 20 but July 8 as the date on which Churchill said this. Anyhow, it is so quotable that Churchill may be forgiven if he came out with it several times, while his listeners nudged one another and whispered, "Famous quotation, eh what?"

21 On August 21, 1621, twelve young women were sent out from England to Virginia, to be sold to bachelors who were looking for wives. The price was 120 pounds of tobacco each, or in other words approximately one pound of tobacco for one pound of woman. "Isn't it romantic!" the dowagers of the colony sighed, as one young man after another staggered up with his load of tobacco, plunked it down, and carried off a giggling bride. Some decided to remain bachelors when they figured out how many smokes they could get out of 120 pounds of Virginia leaf.

Leonardo da Vinci's famous painting, "Mona Lisa" ("La Gioconda"), said to be worth 5 million dollars, was

That silly smirk

stolen from the Louvre Museum in Paris on August 21, 1911. It was recovered two years later from an Italian who said he had taken it because he loved it and could not stand to share it with others. However, after two years of looking at that silly smirk, day after day, he had taken to drink. The painting was returned to the Louvre, and the thief was taken to a mental institution. There, surrounded by calendar art, he gradually returned to normal.

22 On August 22, 1851, the New York Yacht Club's *America* won a race around the Isle of Wight against fourteen yachts belonging to the Royal Yacht Squadron. The English did not challenge the American winners until 1870, when, nineteen years not having been long enough to wait, they lost.

23 The first elevator in a hotel was installed in the six-story Fifth Avenue Hotel, in New York City, on August 23, 1859. Curious hotel guests crowded in for the first ride, those planning to get off on the second floor in the very back and those whose destination was the sixth floor up in front, an arrangement which has remained inviolate.

24 On August 24, in 79 A.D., Mt. Vesuvius erupted and buried Pompeii and Herculaneum. More people know that Bulwer-Lytton wrote a book entitled *The Last Days of Pompeii* than that he himself was very nearly buried at birth under the name Edward George Earle Lytton Bulwer-Lytton. In all fairness, there should also be a book about the last days of Herculaneum.

25 On August 25, 1830, a race took place between a locomotive named "Tom Thumb" and a horse-drawn vehicle. When the locomotive broke down and the horse won, something important was proved. To wit, in a race between a horse-drawn vehicle and a locomotive, the former is sure to win if the latter breaks down.

26 On this day in 1584, says one authority, taking a long chance, was born Frans Hals, the great Dutch portrait and genre painter. Some of the genres he painted are museum pieces. The birthdate of Hals is in dispute, some saying it was not 1584 but c.1580, others that it was *circa* 1580, and still others holding out for 1580(?). It is of no great moment to most of us, though it was unquestionably one of the great moments of the painter's life. His most famous painting is "The Laughing Cavalier," a picture which is not only well painted but well labelled, inasmuch as it depicts a cavalier laughing. This is the sort of thing you don't come upon very often in art.

27 Confucius, the Chinese philosopher, dates from August 27, 551 B.C. To him are attributed such wise sayings as "He who stir tea with chopsticks probably tourist."

28 Radio commercials began in New York on August 28, 1922, advertising a real estate company. Soon you heard such familiar expressions as "But first a word from our sponsor." In time, many radio commercials came to be more stimulating than the programs, but this was not because of any improvement in the commercials.

29 Chop suey was first made in New York City on August 29, 1896, by a Chinese chef who had a lot of leftovers. (See that kindred spirit, Sgt. Dzuba, August 15, above.) He thought it might be something that would appeal to both Chinese and Americans. Or, if neither cared for it, each would think it was what the other liked and do his best to get it down. Chop suey was at that time unknown in China, but it was soon adopted in Peking as an American delicacy and served to tourists from Nebraska who were homesick. "Chop suey" is a Cantonese mispronunciation of two Pekingese words, made with the mouth full of shrimp rice and egg foo yung.

A special occasion

30 On August 30, or possibly 29, in 30 B.C., Cleopatra committed suicide by permitting an asp to bite her. Asps are usually discouraged from taking such liberties, but this was a special occasion. As the asp sank its fangs into Cleopatra's tasty flesh, she is reported to have said something queenly and memorable, such as "Ouch!" The asp said nothing, being too busy. Some believe the asp was an Egyptian cobra; others think it was a viper. Then again it may have been an adder, though how high it could add was anybody's guess. The main thing is that it did the job neatly and quietly.

31 That was the end of Cleopatra, and this is the end of August.

SEPTEMBRIS

S EPTEMBER, *the seventh month of the old Roman year,
got its name from the Latin* septem, *seven. When it
became the ninth month, it retained its original name.
This becomes less and less confusing as fewer and fewer
people know how to count in Latin. Those who believe
September was named after* septum, *a partition inside the
nose, are probably thinking of the Roman nose, in which
it reached its height. The Anglo-Saxons called it Gerst-
monath, barley month, because barley, which was harvested
at this time, could be made into malt and malt into mead.
After a few tankards of mead an Anglo-Saxon trying to say
Gerst-monath was a scream.*

108

1 On September 1, 1878, Emma Nutt (whose parents had thoughtfully kept from naming her Ima) became the first woman telephone operator. Miss Nutt was employed in Boston, where there had been complaints about the rough language used by male operators when the wires became a bit tangled at the switchboard. As for Emma, she not only used ladylike language herself, despite the most trying circumstances, but when she heard abusive epithets from subscribers simply disconnected them until they calmed down. A blasphemous character might shout, "D-mn you! What the h-ll do you mean, keeping me waiting!" But all he would get from Miss Nutt was *click!*

2 Rudolf Friml's operetta, *Rose Marie*, opened in New York on September 2, 1924, and soon every red-blooded male was singing one of its hit tunes, "The Indian Love Call." Occasionally a middle-aged man, not otherwise known for his voice, would burst forth with a rather good baritone while in the tub, where he would sound so much like the hero that he would half expect to hear the answering strains of the Indian maiden and swing into a duet on the chorus.

3 An important stride was made by journalism when, on September 3, 1833, *The New York Sun* became the first successful daily newspaper to sell for a penny. Its publishers could boast, had they thought of it: "Our Two Cents' Worth for Half Price." Since the actual worth of the paper itself, uncontaminated by ink, was more than a penny, the *Sun* might have sold better had its pages been left blank. The first newsboy, we happen to know, was a lad named Barney Flaherty, and it was probably he who coined such words as "wuxtry" and "readalaboudid."

4 The Exchange Buffet, an early form of cafeteria, opened in New York City on September 4, 1885. Picking up a tray as they entered, patrons sidled past the various dishes, carefully selecting more than they could possibly eat. With what they saved by not having to tip, they could buy something at the drugstore to settle their stomachs.

5 On September 5, 1885, Sylvanus F. Bowser of Fort Wayne, Indiana, manufactured the first gasoline pump and delivered it to Jake D. Gumper. Henceforth Jake was known as Gumper the Pumper, which pleased him no end. Service stations were just around the corner (or, more often, *on* the corner), with free air, free water, free maps, free windshield wiping, and free rest rooms. As of this writing, however, owners are still showing a mercenary streak by charging for gasoline and oil.

6 On this day in 1862 occurred the incident on which Whittier's poem about Barbara Frietchie is based. After the Confederates marched into Frederick, Maryland, General Stonewall Jackson is supposed to have ordered soldiers to fire on a Union flag in Mrs. Frietchie's attic window, and they gave it a few bursts. But its owner, not wanting the flag damaged, leaned out the window invitingly, crying, "Shoot, if you must, this old gray head." Observers say that Jackson's men took a shot or two but didn't get even a ricochet. Humiliated because he saw Whittier taking notes, Jackson marched his troops off to target practice.

7 Queen Elizabeth I of England was born on September 7, 1533. She was known as the Virgin Queen, and those who have seen pictures of her, with her long nose and red wig, can understand why.

8 During World War I, on September 8, 1917, the manufacture of whiskey was stopped to conserve grain. This was despite the cogent arguments of those who thought grain might better be saved by stopping the manufacture of bread. Many who had taken only a mild interest in the war now became really incensed at the Kaiser. Look what that Hun was doing to life in America!

9 Almost all the police of Boston walked out on a strike, leaving the city without police protection, on September 9, 1919. The lack of police was noticed at once by proprietors of fruit stands, who were bewildered at being

Police protection

able to sell their choicest peaches and plums instead of having them carried off by the cop on the beat. Gangsters who had paid good money to get the police to lay off them cursed their bad luck. Nobody would buy a ticket to the Policeman's Ball. The strike was ended on September 12, thanks to the firmness of Governor Calvin Coolidge, who would be heard from again, but not at length.

10 A momentous occurrence on September 10, 1927, was the perfection of a frankfurter with a zipper. The manufacturer, an American meat packer, advised consumers to "boil the hot dog in its zippered casing and then discard it." For a while, hot dogs were thrown out with the garbage, and zippered casings, liberally spread with mustard, were manfully downed. Though he made a pilot model, this same manufacturer never quite managed to get a banana with a zipper into commercial production.

11 Jenny Lind, "The Swedish Nightingale," who had come to the United States under the management of P. T. Barnum, opened her American concert series in New York on September 11, 1850. Barnum also brought over Jumbo, the elephant, but not to sing. It was Barnum who said, "A sucker is born every minute," and if this is true, there are plenty of people to fool any time you are so inclined. However, it was not Barnum but Texas Guinan, the night-club entertainer, who greeted patrons with "Hello, sucker!" These easy spenders were pretty gullible during the daytime, too, and may indeed be considered all-day suckers.

12 On September 12, 1922, the Protestant Episcopal House of Bishops voted to take the word "obey" out of the marriage ceremony. A minority report, which has been hushed up, recommended being completely realistic and taking out two other words, "love" and "honor."

13 Defending Gibraltar, the British fought off a vastly superior French and Spanish force on September 13, 1782. What was unusual about this was the technique they used: they dropped red-hot cannon balls on the enemy. It would seem bad enough to be hit by a cold cannon ball. One of the details missing, in the account we read, is whether the British wore gloves.

On September 13, 1931, Rudy Vallee introduced "Life Is Just a Bowl of Cherries" in a musical revue in New York. It was during the Depths of the Depression, and most people, as they listened to Rudy croon, could visualize the bowl, all right, but could see in it only stems and pits.

14 The typewriter ribbon was patented by George K. Anderson of Memphis, Tennessee, on September 14, 1886. Ribbons were installed on the first crude machines with great difficulty, calling for skill and patience on the part of the typist. Despite subsequent improvements in the typewriter, manufacturers have ingeniously contrived to keep installation of the ribbon as difficult as ever. Nowadays a competent typist, who can type sixty or seventy words a minute, needs half an hour to change a typewriter ribbon, including time for the application of cleaning fluid to the hands and lower arms and the filing of broken fingernails. Fingernails may be filed under either *F* or *N*.

This one does something for you

15 This is Felt Hat Day. Practical jokers who find anyone wearing a straw hat crush it down over his ears and ask, "Is it felt?" On this day anyone who hopes to be in style, or wishes to bring happiness to hat manufacturers, haberdashers, and moths, buys a cloth hat. At the clothing store, the salesman is likely to say, "This one *does* something for you," but he is unlikely to be specific about what.

16 King Louis XIV of France was born on September 16, 1638, or September 5 by the Old Style calendar, the one without pictures. He was known as the Sun King, this being the winning entry in the "What Shall We Call the King?" contest, for which any Frenchman was eligible who sent in one franc and the cork from a bottle of *vin ordinaire*. Louis did great and generous things for his people, the most notable being the building of his magnificent palace at Versailles, which anyone was privileged to come and look at any time he wished, as long as he stayed outside the fence. Every time Louis took on a new mistress he added a wing.

17 Failure of new banks, beginning September 17, 1873, led to Black Friday two days later, and the Panic of 1873. The line at the Withdrawals window, instead of being four or five people, stretched out the door, around the corner, and down the street for six blocks. But it was a good day to do business at the Deposits window if you were in a hurry.

18 The cornerstone of the new Capitol was laid by President Washington on September 18, 1793. After the Capitol was burned by the British, another cornerstone was laid by President Madison, in 1818, and when the building was enlarged, in 1851, President Fillmore laid a third cornerstone. Unlike some Presidents, who occasionally lay an egg, these early Chief Executives thought they did their duty when they laid a cornerstone.

19 It was on September 19, 1846, that Elizabeth Barrett escaped from the home of her tyrannical father, at 50 Wimpole Street, London, and went to Italy with Robert Browning. "Boot, saddle, to horse, and away!" cried the virile poet as he galloped across the Channel, with Miss Barrett, her faithful maid Wilson, and her faithful lapdog Flush flung over the saddle. As they galloped (Dirck galloped, Joris galloped, everybody seemed to be out on the road that day), Browning kept his fiancée entertained with cheerful quotations from Browning, such as "Grow old along with me" (not very discreet of him, since he was only thirty-four, while Elizabeth had hit forty) and "Oh, to be in England, now that April's there." Elizabeth, barely up from a sickbed, was lost in her own thoughts. In the haste of their departure, had she remembered all her pills?

20 On September 20, 1881, Vice President Chester A. Arthur took the oath of office after the death of President Garfield. Arthur is well known as the person you forget when you are trying to name all the Presidents of the United States.

21 The famous editorial, "Yes, Virginia, there is a Santa Claus," appeared in *The New York Sun* on September 21, 1897. It was in reply to a letter by eight-year-old Virginia O'Hanlon of New York, who was under pressure from her skeptical contemporaries and trying hard to cling to her faith. What seems a little odd is Virginia's getting fired up about Santa Claus as early as September, unless, as is possible, the merchants had already decorated the downtown streets. In early April of the following year, an editorial entitled "Yes, Shirley, there is an Easter bunny" appeared but failed to stir the public imagination.

22 On September 22, 1692, the last persons were hanged in the American colonies for witchcraft. A few others were condemned but managed to escape, probably on their brooms. A month later, on Halloween, they returned and scared the mush out of the colonists. In olden days, it wasn't easy to tell who was a witch, since everyone wore a high, conical hat with a buckle on it. But if there was someone you didn't like, you could always start a rumor and hope for the best.

Which is witch

23 The first commencement exercises at an American college were held at Harvard on September 23, 1642, professors apparently having taken a long time getting their grades in. The commencement speaker spoke of the challenges awaiting the graduates as they went forth into the world, no doubt having in mind the Indians lurking behind every tree and bush. He stressed the usefulness of their liberal arts education, with its emphasis on Latin, Greek, philosophy, and literature, pointing out how helpful this would be in tilling a rocky New England farm. The only thing that curtailed the eloquence of his speech was his inability to quote from Washington, Jefferson, and Lincoln.

24 Another Black Friday (see September 17, above) occurred on September 24, 1869, when Jay Gould tried to corner the gold market. What this makes abundantly clear is that September is a bad month to get mixed

117

up with financiers. On Fridays, especially, you should draw all your money out of the bank, put it under your pillow, and stay in bed.

25 Sequoia National Park, in California, was established by Congress on September 25, 1890. Congress takes a good deal of credit for this, but it should be noted that the giant redwood trees and other scenic features were already there. Now, however, these are embellished by fences, foresters, and signs reading "You Are Entering Sequoia National Park," "You Are Leaving Sequoia National Park," and "Rubbish."

26 "Johnny Appleseed," famous in American folklore for planting thousands of apple trees, was born on September 26, 1774. Actually he was more a hayseed than an Appleseed, and was named John Chapman. He had an odd, but nonetheless fruitful, compulsion to spread sunshine by planting shade trees. Each time he ate an apple he carefully saved the seeds, which he carried around in his pocket and planted wherever he saw a bare spot. Soon apple trees were springing up in people's lawns, in the middle of roads, and in houses with dirt floors. Johnny wanted people to have plenty of apples, which they could pick one at a time, fresh from the tree. As he said, with some truth, "An apple a day keeps."

27 Book matches were patented on September 27, 1892, by Joshua Pusey of Lima, Pennsylvania. On hearing the news, zealots were overjoyed, thinking Mr. Pusey had invented a book that could be scratched and set fire to, thus greatly expediting bookburning. They were doomed to disappointment.

28 On September 28, 1751, George Washington, then nineteen, made his only sea voyage, to the Barbados. Not only did he get seasick, but he contracted smallpox, which marked him for life. Later, on his famous crossing of the Delaware, he was feeling none too good when he stood up to have his portrait painted, as the picture reveals.

29 Lord Nelson, the English admiral, was born on September 29, 1758. He had only one good eye, which is why, at Trafalgar, he used a telescope instead of binoculars. Much has been written about Lord Nelson and Lady Hamilton, and it takes considerable restraint not to write more.

30 It could be September 30, or any day late in the month, with which the famous painting "September Morn," painted in 1911 by French artist Paul Chabas, is concerned. It shows a nude young woman standing in water half way up to her knees and clutching herself in such a way as either to keep herself warm or to get by the censor. The water looks cold and uninviting, suggesting that the young woman has gone on a late vacation, perhaps taking advantage of out-of-season rates, and has further cut down expenses by not buying a bathing suit. The beach looks deserted, but will not be for long.

OCTOBRIS

Octomber, the eighth month of the old Roman year, was temporarily renamed several times, to honor such emperors as Germanicus and Herculeus. It was even named Faustinus, in honor of Faustina, the wife of Emperor Antoninus, which was sweet of the emperor and cheaper than building her a triumphal arch or an aqueduct. Things were in a state of flux for a while, and it must have been pretty upsetting to be told, "I'll pay you back the first of Germanicus," and then when that time of year came around find it was Herculeus or Faustinus and be laughed at when you tried to collect. There is a poem about October by George Cooper, the man who wrote "Sweet Genevieve," that begins:

> October gave a party;
>   The leaves by hundreds came:
> The ashes, oaks, and maples,
>   And those of every name.

It was a gay crowd, for nobody enjoys a party as much as a leaf, dancing around on its little stem and so full of chlorophyll that even if it perspires it never offends.

1 The first monument to a bird in the United States was unveiled at Salt Lake City on October 1, 1913. It commemorated the sea gulls that came from the Great Salt Lake, in 1848, and attacked the grasshoppers that were destroying the fields of Mormon settlers. (It was not that they meant any harm; they were just hungry.) Since birds usually perch all over monuments of people, it would be tit for tat if people were to perch all over this monument to birds. We have not done any research into monuments to grasshoppers.

2 On October 2, 1882, William H. Vanderbilt, the railroad magnate, made the headlines with his famous remark, "The public be damned!" The only thing newsworthy about this remark was its being made in the presence of newspaper reporters. Vanderbilt had been asked whether he operated his railroads for the public benefit. He had never heard of such a silly question and, naturally, exploded. A very rich man, he could afford anything, including, it seems, being frank.

3 Another famous remark is said to have been made on October 3, 1919, on the occasion of the visit of the King and Queen of Belgium to New York City. The Queen having said something now completely forgotten, Mrs. John F. Hylan, the wife of the Mayor of New York, replied, "Queenie, you said a mouthful!" The Queen's comment on Mrs. Hylan's comment was in French, and has been variously translated as "Who is that dreadful creature?" and "Get me out of here."

4 In a letter to his son, on October 4, 1752, Lord Chesterfield wrote, "I am going to bed, just at the hour at which I suppose you are beginning to live." Chesterfield, only fifty-eight but feeling seventy, was at Bath, taking the waters. He had had about all he could take. Instead of feeling younger, he felt bloated, and wanted to tell his son a few things before it was too late (i.e., 10:00 P.M.). As for that young rakehell, he was in Berlin, having himself a ball. When his father's letter of advice arrived, he carefully placed it on his desk with all the others he was too busy to read.

5 The first baby show was held in Springfield, Ohio, on October 5, 1854, with 127 babies entered. The judges escaped unharmed by giving 127 prizes. One of the judges, who was not asked back the next year, later described a baby as "an alimentary canal with a loud noise at one end and no sense of responsibility at the other."

6 On October 6, 1863, a Turkish bath, the first in America, opened in Brooklyn, New York. Whoever introduced this contraption from Turkey was unable to read the directions, and therefore did not realize that it was an ancient instrument of torture, used by the sultans to force confessions from spies and traitors. The only reason they were called baths was that in them people came clean. A certain amount of efficiency was achieved when it was discovered that they could be used simultaneously for steaming clams. Along with the Turkish bath came the Turkish towel, a coarse cloth which proved excellent for removing sweat, grime, and skin.

7 James Whitcomb Riley, the Hoosier poet, was born on October 7, 1849. (When someone says, questioningly, "Hoosier poet?" you are not supposed to reply, "I dunno. Who's yours?") Among Riley's best-loved poems is "Little Orphant Annie," which contains such immortal lines as:

> His Mammy heered him holler, an' his Daddy
> heered him bawl,
> An' when they turn't the kivvers down, he wasn't
> there at all.

But people ain't a-readin' Riley the way they ust to.

By coincidence, on the very day James Whitcomb Riley was born, Edgar Allan Poe died. This is the sort of thing that keeps the literary population on an even keel, and we should be grateful.

8 On October 8, 1871, the great fire of Chicago broke out when a cow kicked over a lantern in Mrs. O'Leary's barn. Chicagoans have been taking it out on cows ever since, at the stockyards. One of the questions that naturally arises about the famous holocaust is why Mrs.

Mrs. O'Leary's cow

O'Leary thought it necessary to leave a lantern by the cow. Did she think the creature might want to get up in the night? This, in the opinion of some, is carrying kindness to animals too far.

9 What Mrs. O'Leary's cow would probably have liked was an electric blanket, but this was not available until October 9, 1940, when it was manufactured by the Simmons Company at Petersburg, Virginia. We have it on reliable authority that the number of persons who have been electrocuted by electric blankets is negligible. Recent models are equipped with an interesting safety feature: a slit through which the user, if he has left the thermostat on too high, will pop up in the middle of the night like a piece of toast.

10 On October 10, 1865, John Wesley Hyatt won a
$10,000 prize by producing the best substitute for
an ivory billiard ball. Even an elephant couldn't tell the
difference. The next step, of course, was to make imitation
Ivory soap, the old soap of genuine ivory being inclined to
sink. It got so an idealist could never be sure he wasn't living in an ivory tower made of plastic.

11 A radio singer, Vaughn De Leath, in her program
on October 11, 1921, introduced a type of singing
called "crooning." Few (and now you are one of the few)
are aware that the word derives from the Icelandic *krauna*,
meaning "murmur." Torch singers are especially popular
at parties in Iceland, where they are good for breaking the
ice. In our own country, crooning has been a great help to
persons who wish to get rich and famous from singing but
have no voice.

12 On October 12, 1492, Christopher Columbus discovered America or, according to the followers of
Leif Ericson, rediscovered it. The Great Navigator landed
on the east coast of the Bahamas and was not more than
10,000 miles from where he thought he was.

13 This is National Grandparents Day. Let us pay
tribute to those dear sweet people, especially the
ones who have homes of their own and come to visit only
when they are urgently needed. One day a year would not
seem to be overdoing it.

14 On October 14, 1066, at the Battle of Hastings, William of Normandy, the bastard, defeated King Harold and his English forces. This made 1066 a famous date, and won William the title of William the Conqueror and Harold the title of Last of the Saxon Kings. One of the most interesting figures of the battle was Taillefer, a juggling minstrel who led the Normans, tossing his sword into the air and singing catchy tunes about Charlemagne and Roland the while. The matter-of-fact English were unimpressed by this diversion. They thought Taillefer's conduct unbecoming a soldier and only fair for a poet. So they clobbered him with a stone axe and ran him through with a spear. Let this be a lesson to drum majorettes with literary aspirations.

Musing among the ruins

15 While musing among the ruins of Rome, on October 15, 1764, Edward Gibbon conceived the project which led to *The Decline and Fall of the Roman Empire*. The sixth and final volume appeared in 1788, twenty-four years after that lucky day among the ruins. Gibbon, a morbid fellow, enjoyed every minute of it. It was he who defined history as "little more than the crimes, follies, and misfortunes of mankind," and it is no wonder his favorite historical personage was a decadent Roman, trying desperately to squeeze in a few more orgies before the place was sacked by the Goths.

16 On October 16, 1846, a demonstration of painless surgery was given. It took place at Massachusetts General Hospital (hence the term "general anesthetic"), and the surgeon was Dr. John C. Warren. Other Boston physicians, having an afternoon off and not playing golf, watched from the gallery. Though they had been skeptical at first, when the operation was over they applauded so loudly that they woke the patient.

17 It was on October 17, 1869, that Henry M. Stanley was sent off by the *New York Herald* to find the missing Scottish missionary, David Livingstone. Two years later, on November 10, 1871, Stanley met Livingstone face to face in Ujiji, Central Africa. Think of the difference it would have made to Stanley's fame had he said something like "Hi, there" or "How's it in Ujiji?" instead of "Dr. Livingstone, I presume?" The good doctor, his mouth full of flavorsome roots, made no memorable remark, but merely nodded.

18 The Mason-Dixon Line was established between Pennsylvania and Maryland on October 18, 1767, by two English surveyors who, by an odd coincidence, were named Mason and Dixon. Everything north of the line came to be known as the North and everything south as the

South. What this country has always needed is a line down the middle so we could be sure of what is the East and what is the West. This could lead to all sorts of interesting possibilities, such as another Civil War, fought in a different direction.

19 On October 19, 1860, Abraham Lincoln, who was then clean shaven, replied to an eleven-year-old girl who thought it would help him win the presidential election if he grew a beard. Lincoln rejected the suggestion, not wishing to change all those campaign posters. But the idea seems to have grown on him, along with his whiskers, or maybe he ran out of razor blades. Regardless of what his beard may have done for Lincoln, it has been a great help to character actors who have played the part. Otherwise they would have had to rely on a stovepipe hat and a shawl.

20 General Douglas MacArthur, who had been forced to leave Corregidor two years before, came back to the Philippines on October 20, 1944. Waiting only to be sure the public address system was working, he said tersely, "I have returned." Some may have got the erroneous impression from the first person singular that General MacArthur was alone. Actually, he was accompanied by a number of American soldiers, sailors, and marines.

21 Samuel Taylor Coleridge, the author of "The Rime of the Ancient Mariner" and other poems, was born on October 21, 1772. "The Rime of the Ancient Mariner" contains the famous

> Water, water, everywhere,
> Nor any drop to drink,

which is often misquoted "And not a drop to drink." By correcting those who make this vulgar error, and doing the same to those who mess up Shakespeare's "All that glisters is not gold," you can perform a service to literature and win the undying dislike of everyone who hears you.

Rugged individualist

22 In a speech on October 22, 1928, Secretary of Commerce Herbert Hoover, campaigning for the Presidency, coined the phrase "rugged individualism." What he meant, as he proved by personal example, was the courage to go on wearing high stiff collars long after they were out of fashion, just because they were uncomfortable.

23 You probably have no idea what Blanche S. Scott is famous for. Well, on October 23, 1910, at Fort Wayne, Indiana, she became the first woman to make a public airplane flight by herself. Miss Scott rose to a height of 12 feet, but came down after a short while for some unexplained reason—perhaps because she had no oxygen mask.

24 Anna Edson Taylor on October 24, 1901, went over Niagara Falls in a barrel, thus fulfilling a lifetime ambition. Mrs. Taylor, a schoolteacher who probably wanted to get away from the classroom, had the barrel fixed up quite comfortably, with pillows and suchlike, and by pressing her eye against the bunghole could see everything and at the same time keep the water out. When they fished her out and opened the barrel, she had hardly a bruise, except an unusual circular one around her right eye.

25 On October 25, 1854, occurred the Charge of the Light Brigade, which brought fame to Alfred, Lord Tennyson. "Half a league, half a league, half a league onward," Tennyson began his poem, giving readers the impression of having difficulty getting started. "Someone had blundered," he wrote, naming no names unless there was a chap in the War Office named Someone. The charge, which took place in the Crimean War, proved conclusively that it is safer to write about a battle than to be in it.

26 It is said that on October 26, 1667, King Charles II of England got his first taste of cranberries. Seafarers, returning from Cape Cod, brought ten barrels to the royal household, and for a few days they were running out of the King's ears. (Some thought he was bleeding to death.) Charles was a man of almost no self-restraint, and if he acted like this over his first taste of cranberries, just think of those first weeks with poor Nell Gwyn. It was

King Charles and Nell

Charles who, on his deathbed, apologized to his courtiers for taking such a long time dying. He must have sensed their impatience, or perhaps he noticed James II, out in the hall, trying on the crown.

27 William Marcy ("Boss") Tweed, the head of Tammany Hall, was arrested on October 27, 1871, for defrauding New York City of millions of dollars. (Some sources say October 26, instead of October 27, which leads one to wonder whether he was arrested at midnight.) "Why did you do it, Boss?" his heartbroken henchmen asked when they visited him in his cell. What they meant was, why did he let himself be caught. Whether tweed, a rough, scratchy cloth, is named after Tweed, or Tweed is named after tweed, we have not tried to find out. Anyhow, they are as alike as Tweedledum and Tweedledee, who were probably named after each other.

28 The Italian Fascists left their headquarters in Naples and began their march on Rome on October 28, 1922. They wore black shirts to cut down on laundry while traveling. Mussolini himself, not sure how things would go in Rome, came up later by train, thereby instituting a new order: (1) followers, (2) leader.

29 Sir Walter Raleigh was executed in London on October 29, 1618. He had lived many years in the Tower, where he wrote, among other things, a *History of the World*. It is doubtful whether he could have composed such a monumental work without the quiet of prison, and also without a better-than-average prison library. It might be added that Raleigh spelled his name several different ways, but never Shakespeare. After a few years of experimentation, he settled down to Ralegh, which he obviously preferred, but he is in the minority.

30 On October 30, 1938, Orson Welles frightened the wits out of radio listeners by broadcasting a dramatization of H. G. Wells's *The War of the Worlds*. It described an invasion by men from Mars, and was so realistic that even those who scoffed at it did so from a safe place under the bed. Afterward, those who had not tuned in were quick to tell those who had that *they* would not have been panicked by a little old radio broadcast. It can be confidently expected that when the men from Mars really do invade this planet, everyone will turn off his radio and say, "Haven't they anything better than a rerun of that old Orson Welles thing?"

31   On the last day of the month, in 1517, Martin Luther nailed his ninety-five theses to the door of the church in Wittenberg, Germany. It must have been an enormous door. Generally it is advisable, or at least thoughtful, to use thumbtacks instead of nails. But Luther wanted to gather a crowd, and people came from every part of town to see what all the pounding was about. What we have always wondered is whether Luther ever hit his finger and, if so, what he said.

NOVEMBRIS

NOVEMBER *was the ninth month in the old Roman year. When it became the eleventh month, the Senate considered renaming it in honor of Tiberius, whose birthday was on the sixteenth. But Tiberius, one of the smarter of the Roman emperors, recognized flattery when he saw it. "What's on your minds, boys?" he asked. "Trying to get my help at the next election?" The Senators, caught flat-footed, changed the subject and shuffled out.*

The Anglo-Saxons had two names for November, Windmonath, "wind month," and Blodmonath, "blood month," the latter because of a seasonal upsurge in murders. Thomas Hood has caught the spirit of the month in his lilting lines:

> No warmth, no cheerfulness, no healthful ease,
>   No comfortable feel in any member—
> No shade, no shine, no butterflies, no bees,
>   No fruits, no flowers, no leaves, no birds,
>   November!

Notice the lift you get out of that final exclamation point. The poem, by the way, is called "No," and leaves the reader with several deep thoughts, such as what a sad state the world is in without a single vember.

1 On November 1, 1939, a rabbit reproduced by artificial impregnation was exhibited to the New York Academy of Medicine. The little bunny had no idea why it was such a celebrity or, for that matter, who its father was. Despite the success of the experiment, the technique never seemed to appeal to rabbits.

2 Fingerprinting in Federal penitentiaries began November 2, 1904, in the United States Penitentiary at Leavenworth, Kansas. As each con's fingers were inked and then, one by one, pressed down on a sheet of paper, the trusty in charge would recite, in his most jovial manner:

> This little piggy went to market,
>   This little piggy stayed home,
> This little piggy left fingerprints
>   On a safe made of steel and chrome.

Handcuffed as they were, convicts had trouble getting their inky hands around the trusty's neck, but finally managed. They were not prosecuted.

3 The world organization of the Woman's Christian Temperance Union was established at a convention in Detroit on November 3, 1883. Members of the WCTU became intemperate only on the subject of intemperance, which sent them into a rage. "Lips that touch liquor," said one of them, quoting George W. Young, "must never touch mine." At eighty-three, she had little to fear.

4 Though artificial legs had been used previously, on November 4, 1846, Benjamin F. Palmer of Meredith, New Hampshire, produced a leg with a revolutionary feature. It had a joint that was guaranteed to work noiselessly! This is more than can be said for some of us who creak embarrassingly when we get up after sitting a little too long. Mr. Palmer, an ingenious man, had thus improved on nature, which is no small trick.

5 On November 5, 1605, Guy Fawkes was completing preparations to blow up the House of Lords while King James I and all the top men were assembled there. He had filled the basement with gunpowder (no one interfered, thinking it coal, albeit rather finely ground), and he was just about to light the fuse when seized. It was a narrow escape for everyone, including Guy, who might have blown himself up, had anything gone wrong, instead of getting off with torture, hanging, and dismemberment. If the Gunpowder Plot had succeeded, there would have been the most thorough reshuffling of the government in English history. As it was, all the conspirator accomplished was the addition of another holiday, Guy Fawkes Day, an interesting instance of a man being remembered for what he failed to do.

6 The first formal (black tie?) intercollegiate football game was played on November 6, 1869, between Princeton and Rutgers. Each team was made up of twenty-five men. The winning team was thus able to tear down the goal posts without any help from the spectators, simply by surging over them en masse. Those were the days!

7 The elephant was first used as the emblem of the Republican Party in a cartoon in *Harper's Weekly* on November 7, 1874. It was drawn by Thomas Nast, but was not as nasty as some versions that have appeared since. Republicans say that the elephant was chosen as their symbol because an elephant never forgets, except maybe a few items like the Teapot Dome Scandal. The Democrats, on the other hand, chose as their emblem the donkey, doubtless after looking up the dictionary definitions: "1. an ass. 2. a stupid, silly, or obstinate person."

8 On November 8, 1793, the Louvre Museum in Paris was opened to the public. It was originally built as a royal residence in 1204, and gradually expanded by a succession of monarchs to make room for additional nudes, some of them on canvas. The art collection was increased by Francis I, who gave his soldiers a check list so that they would know what to take from museums in neighboring countries, and not loot tastelessly. Not until 1793, with the coming of the Republic, were these art treasures made available to the common people, who could wander through the enormous building for hours and hours, looking for a place to sit.

9 This is the birthdate, in 1853, of Stanford White, the famous American architect who was even more famous for having been murdered in Madison Square Garden on June 25, 1906, by Harry K. Thaw. Thaw shot him because he thought the architect had designs on his wife, showgirl Evelyn Nesbit, and he wasn't going to have her used as drawing paper. The best thing that came out of the murder trial was Wilson Mizner's remark when he observed a particularly rococo building nearing completion. "My God!" he exclaimed, "Thaw shot the wrong architect."

10 *Floradora*, the musical hit by Leslie Stuart, opened in New York on November 10, 1900. It featured the Floradora Sextette, six beautiful girls who sang and danced and, with reckless abandon, winked at men on the front row. There was a great deal of wickedness in 1900, which is why those who graduated from college in this year

Naughty naught

were said to be in the class of Naughty Naught. Queen Victoria was on her last legs, which she kept well covered, and it was probably the news of such goings-on that killed her in 1901. The Floradora Sextette, by the way, stopped the show with "Tell Me Pretty Maiden," a real sizzler, and daringly twirled their parasols the while. "What is the world coming to?" respectable people asked, and it is perhaps just as well they never knew.

11 On November 11, 1926, education in America started on the long downhill road when the Board of Regents of the University of Wisconsin approved academic credit for a course in dancing. One of the problems taken up in the course was what to do when a woman insists on leading ("Bend her right wrist back until it snaps"). Another was what to say when you slip on an over-waxed floor and you and your partner go down hard ("Oops! Sorry."). The course was offered by the Department of Physical Education and could be substituted for Advanced Shot Putting if there was a conflict.

This is also Armistice Day, later called Veterans' Day to honor those who had gone through several years of watching Armistice Day parades and listening to Armistice Day speeches.

In England, on November 11, at least at Fenny Stratford, near Bletchley, Buckinghamshire, the vicar sets off six small cannons (and we like to think that the canon sets off six small vicars) in a ceremony known as "Firing the Fenny Poppers." Natives have long since forgotten why this is done, but everyone seems to get a bang out of it.

12 An "autobank" was established on November 12, 1946, by the Exchange National Bank of Chicago. Henceforth you could transact business without leaving your car, or in other words stand in line sitting down. You could also honk at those who were taking too long at the teller's window, which had not been possible before unless you carried a horn.

13 *The Sheik*, starring Rudolph Valentino, was shown in New York theaters on November 13, 1921. Women in the audience swooned, carried off by their emotions while imagining themselves carried off by Valentino. Ushers, dressed like sheiks, rode up and down the aisles on Arabian steeds, bringing smelling salts. Most women stayed to see the picture a second time, wishing to see the part they had missed while they were unconscious.

By dropping dry-ice pellets from an airplane into a cloud, scientists produced artificial snow over Mt. Greylock, Massachusetts on November 13, 1946. Far below, the pilot saw little men with snow shovels shaking their fists and cursing him. Thus have all great innovations been received.

14 The world's first streetcar appeared in New York City on November 14, 1832. It is described as having been "drawn by horses on tracks," a method soon given up when the streetcar was put on the tracks instead of the horses, which kept slipping off. Horses were later supplanted by electricity, which made possible greater speed and the expression "You're off your trolley."

15 On this day in 1806 Zebulon Pike, attempting to discover the source of the Mississippi River, sighted the mountain peak that came to be called "Pike's Peak." For those who demand freedom of choice, it is called "Pike's Peak or Bust." Interestingly, and rather sadly, Pike himself tried to reach the peak but failed, largely because he took the wrong path and wound up on the top of another mountain. Whether he ever found the source of the Mississippi we don't know, but from this it appears unlikely.

16 The American Association for the Advancement of Atheism was incorporated in New York State on November 16, 1925. By outdoing Alcoholics Anonymous and the Automobile Association of America, the AAAA gained first place in the telephone book. Its members kept close watch over one another to prevent backsliding, such as furtively slipping into church for a quick one.

The change at the Palace Theater in New York, on November 16, 1932, from vaudeville to moving pictures signalled the doom of vaudeville. Many performers, unable to wait until 1948 and the Ed Sullivan Show on TV, were thrown out of work, and there is nothing so sad as an unemployed fire eater, down to his last match, unless it is a dummy who cannot afford a ventriloquist.

17 A course for dental hygienists was inaugurated by Dr. Alfred C. Fones at the Fones Clinic in Bridgeport, Connecticut, on November 17, 1913. Thirty-three young women enrolled and were taught such things as

Which instrument to hand

which instrument to hand the dentist when he absent-mindedly asks for his seven iron and how to frisk departing patients for magazines. After each lesson they tied a piece of dental floss around the left index finger to help them remember. This was especially useful in helping them remember which was their left index finger.

18 The Female Charitable Society of Wiscosset, Maine, meeting on November 18, 1805, became the first woman's club in the United States. The husbands of the members became aware of the club that evening, when their wives returned home too late to prepare dinner, and so full of cookies and tea that they couldn't see why their husbands wanted anything to eat, anyhow.

19 Leopold von Auenbrugger, the Viennese physician, was born on November 19, 1722. It was he who discovered the percussion method of diagnosing pulmonary diseases. "Say '*Ach*,' " he would tell his patients, and thump them on the chest while listening through a stethoscope. An after-hours drummer in a Viennese combo, he would sometimes get carried away by his beat and leave his patient badly bruised. Fortunately, he was every bit as good at the treating of bruises as he was at diagnosing lung ailments.

20 Effective November 20, 1914, all American citizens were required to submit photographs to be attached to their passports. They were not permitted to submit a photo of their own choice, but were to have one made at a nearby shop which specialized in thugs, imbeciles, and corpses. Quite obviously the photographs were not intended for identification but for relaxing international tensions by giving French and Italian customs inspectors a laugh.

21 On November 21, 1871, a cigar lighter was patented by Moses F. Gale of New York City. The first cigar lighter was a gas jet that invariably worked, because it remained on. It would not only light cigars but singe mustaches and set fire to celluloid collars. A customer, before lighting up, would run a cigar back and forth under his nose, remove the band, and test for draw, all the time being watched anxiously by the proprietor. Meanwhile, out in front, the cigar store wooden Indian stood as impassively as a wooden Indian, a tomahawk in one hand and a half dozen cigars in the other. An Indian who forgot which hand was which, in the heat of battle, would sometimes clobber his foe with a two-for-a-quarter Perfecto.

22 The SOS distress signal was adopted on November 22, 1906, to replace the old CQD signal. The trouble with CQD was that radio operators had been failing to put the little tail on the bottom of the Q, and it looked like COD. As for SOS, it was popularly thought to mean Save Our Ship, though it could just as well have meant Swim Over, Somebody. The SOS signal was not sent from an American ship until August 11, 1909, when the CQS signal was also sent. When your ship is about to go down, you can't be too sure, and there were probably those aboard, not trusting radio signals, who yelled, "Help!"

The Archer

On November 22 the sun enters the sign of the zodiac known as Sagittarius, or the Archer. This sign, said to be named for the Babylonian god of war, shows a centaurlike figure, part horse and part man, shooting an arrow. Fortunately for the Archer, the horse part is in the rear and the man part is in front; if it were the other way around it would be virtually impossible to draw a bow or do anything more warlike than whinny. One thing about Sagittarius: when he was called a horse's ass he merely shrugged his shoulders and muttered the Babylonian equivalent of *"C'est la vie."*

23 Enrico Caruso, the Italian tenor, made his American debut at the Metropolitan Opera House on November 23, 1903. He sang the role of the Duke in *Rigoletto*, holding the high notes until many in the audience shouted, "Bravo!" and "Bravissimo!" and then, growing worried, "That's long enough, Enrico." Never had such clear, bell-like tones been heard, except from a bell. Caruso was widely known because of his records, not all of which were for the length of time he could hold a note.

24 Charles Darwin's *The Origin of Species* was published on November 24, 1859. This famous book is concerned with the descent of man, a descent that continues apace. The descent of man, it should be noted, has been matched by that of woman. Other fascinating books by Darwin include *Climbing Plants,* which tells how to shinny up a beanstalk, and the even more engrossing *Formation of Vegetable Mould through the Action of Worms,* the Bible of worm-watchers.

25 In James Boswell's journal for November 25, 1762, he makes this plaintive statement: "I have now been some time in town (London) without female sport." For a sportsman like young Boswell, this was a sad state of affairs. But expectation of what might happen any night now is why the reader keeps pressing on, and why *Boswell's London Journal* became a best-seller 200 years later.

26   This is one of the days in National Bird Cage Week. Another source calls it National Caged Bird Week. This is the sort of thing that can make a great deal of difference to you, especially if you are a bird.

27   On November 27, 1908, Dr. Charles W. Eliot, president of Harvard University, completed editing the *Harvard Classics*. This work, which runs to fifty volumes, is better known as *The Five-Foot Shelf*, and is fine for those who like to read so many inches a month. Anyone who has read the whole thing, from beginning to end, will probably tell you.

28   Ferdinand Magellan on November 28, 1520, entered the Pacific Ocean on his way around the world. He was often in difficulty (see the straits of Magellan), and during the ninety-eight-day crossing of the Pacific was re-

Often in difficulty

duced to eating oxhides, sawdust, and rats. One can imagine Magellan's cabin boy sticking his head into the galley and shouting to the cook, "One rodent medium rare, and a side order of sawdust!" But Magellan made it, arriving in what is now the Philippines and receiving the customary reward of explorers: he was killed by natives.

29 A Committee of Secret Correspondence was organized by the American colonists on November 29, 1775, to write things about the British that were not wholly complimentary. Invisible ink was used, and British officials who steamed open envelopes were puzzled at how much blank paper was being sent back and forth. After the Revolutionary War broke out, and censorship grew even tighter, the members of the Committee felt the need for additional security measures, such as invisible paper. But the colonists had the right idea. They knew that whenever you want to perform a lot of work without any visible results, the thing to do is to form a committee.

On November 29, 1929, Richard E. Byrd flew over the South Pole (in a plane). Since he had already flown over the North Pole on May 9, 1926, he become the first man to fly over both the North and South Poles, a distinction which has created considerable envy, especially among those of us who have never flown over even one Pole, except maybe as we passed over the Pittsburgh area.

30 In Turin, Italy, on November 30, 1922, the great actress Sarah Bernhardt, who though not shy was always retiring, made her final final appearance.

DECEMBRIS

DECEMBER, *named after the Latin* decem, *was orig-inally the tenth month, when it was beginning to get cool enough for the Romans to switch from cold baths to hot.The abbreviation for December is Dec., which reminds us that there is no abbreviation for May, and also that May is Yam when spelled backward, which makes more sense than Rebmeced. This suggests a poem for re-membering lengths of the months:*

> *Thirty days hath Rebmetpes,*
>   *Lirpa, Enuj, and Rebmevon.*
> *All the rest, save Yraurbef,*
>   *Have thirty-one, like Tsugua.*

This would be even better if it rhymed, but you can't have everything.

1 It is believed that the first skywriting in the United States was accomplished on December 1, 1922, by Captain Cyril Turner, of the Royal Air Force. He wrote "HELLO USA," no doubt choosing this message because there were no i's to dot or t's to cross.

2 On December 2, 1804, Napoleon Bonaparte formally became Emperor of France. Just as the Pope was about to place the crown (made of gold laurel leaves, guaranteed not to wilt) on the Emperor's head, Napoleon grabbed it and crowned himself. The *klonk* could be heard throughout the Cathedral of Notre Dame, and the crowd of onlookers, after a moment of concern, laughed uneasily. Was Napoleon impatient? A do-it-yourself type? A show-off hamming it up? You can imagine how the Pope felt, after practicing his part for days.

Do-it-yourself coronation

3 The first successful Technicolor motion picture was *The Toll of the Sea*, shown at the Rialto Theater in New York City on December 3, 1922. You could see the green of the ocean and of the faces of people on shipboard. Standing outside at the conclusion of the picture, a dejected poet wrote:

> After views
> In Technicolor,
> Nature's hues
> Seem somewhat duller.

4 The National Grange of the Patrons of Husbandry was founded on December 4, 1867. It is usually called simply the Grange, to avoid any connection with the rival organization, the Patrons of Wifery. Red Grange, by the way, was a famous football player and not a communist cell in the organization.

A dramatization of Erskine Caldwell's novel *Tobacco Road* opened on Broadway on December 4, 1933. You had only to see those sharecroppers lined up along the edge, full of great expectorations, to understand how the road got its name. As one of the characters said of a barefoot lad, "He's the spittin' image of his paw."

5 The first nudist organization in America was the American League for Physical Culture, established in New York City on December 5, 1929. The League was organized by three men, who soon decided it might be more educational if it were coeducational. Because it was December when the League was organized, its members did not go outdoors for some months, but just sat huddled around the steam pipes in a Lexington Avenue basement. In June, however, they had their first nudist summer camp, at Central Valley, New York, which almost overnight became a popular area for picnickers and bird-watchers. One problem faced by scholarly nudists was where to carry their Phi Beta Kappa keys, this learned society having been founded, by coincidence, on December 5, 1776.

6 On December 6, 1882, the planet Venus passed across the sun, something that doesn't happen every day. This is next scheduled for June 8, 2004, and you might make note of it. To protect your eyes, be sure to look through a piece of smoked glass.

7 The Watch and Ward Society of Boston on December 7, 1908, successfully prosecuted a book salesman who had offered copies of Elinor Glyn's spicy book, *Three Weeks*. This was the beginning of the phrase "banned in Boston," which came to mean more to an impoverished author than the Pulitzer Prize.

8 The American Bird Banding Association was formed on December 8, 1909, by an enthusiastic group of bird-banders. They had been banding individually, but now decided to band together. As for the technique involved, once you have a bird in hand (and you know what a bird in hand is worth), the rest is easy, provided you also have a band in hand. The bird, by the way, will have some explaining to do on returning to the flock, with friends forever waddling up, asking, "What did you do to your leg?"

9 Along about now, if not sooner, people start singing Christmas carols. One of the favorites is "Silent Night"—something you are not likely to enjoy, because of lusty-lunged carollers, until the twenty-sixth.

10 Emily Dickinson, the American poet, was born on December 10, 1830. She wrote nearly two thousand poems, but only seven were published in her lifetime. This was not because of rejection by editors, which is what happens to most poets, but because she wrote just for kicks. Besides, she didn't want to go to the bother of submitting things, which meant enclosing a self-addressed stamped envelope. A sample of her more difficult poetry is

> I'm nobody. Who are you?
> Are you nobody, too?

Makes you think, doesn't it?

Southern benefactor

11 Not until December 11, 1919, at Enterprise, Alabama, was a monument erected, somewhat tardily, to an insect. In this instance it was dedicated to the boll weevil, which caused such destruction to cotton crops that many farmers gave up their farms and went to the city, where they became rich. Such an important contribution to the economy of the South could not be overlooked, and a monument seemed just the thing. Besides, it provided a hard surface on which to crush weevils that were clinging to the cotton and having themselves a boll.

12 In Vienna, on December 12, 1792, Ludwig van Beethoven took his first music lesson from Franz Joseph Haydn. When Ludwig came into the parlor, he did not at once see his teacher, who was inside the clavier, tuning it up. "Where are you Haydn?" he asked. "I'm not Haydn," said Haydn, "I'm here." It was quite a while before the confusion was resolved and the lesson could begin. Some think the incident suggested the famous "Who's on first?" routine of comics Abbott and Costello, but it must have been funnier in German, with two musicians.

13 It is odd that no one had ever done it before, but on December 13, 1920, at Mount Wilson Observatory in California, Dr. F. G. Pease measured a fixed star. The star was Betelgeuse, and using some other means, surely, than a ruler, or even a yardstick, Dr. Pease found it to be 260,000,000 miles in diameter. What surprised people was that the measurement came out an even number of miles, right on the nose. Of course, Betelgeuse is a fixed star, and there is no telling how large it was, or even what shape, before it was fixed. Whoever fixes stars does a good job on them, because afterward they look as good as new, at least from a distance.

14 On December 14, 1882, Senator George G. Vest of Missouri, in a speech against woman's suffrage, brought down the house (no, it was the Senate) with his oft-quoted declaration: "Woman's place is in the home!" Senator Vest is even more widely known for his touching

Eulogy on the Dog, in which he used all the flattering adjectives he withheld from his speech on women. Had someone introduced a bill giving the vote to Fido, the Senator would have been for it.

15 Perhaps you have never wondered who was the first reigning monarch to visit the United States. Well, you should have. It was David Kalakaua, King of the Sandwich Islands, who was received at the White House by President Grant on December 15, 1874. Grant gave King Kalakaua a picture of himself leading the troops at Vicksburg in a Union suit, and the King presented Grant with a hand-carved replica of the original sandwich.

16 The Boston Tea Party took place on December 16, 1773. The colonists showed their spirit of independence by taking their tea with lemon instead of cream and sugar. As a final gesture of insult to the British, they threw their cups and saucers into Boston Harbor, creating a hazard to navigation.

17 The one-way street came into being in traffic regulations established in New York City on December 17, 1791. While we do not know who was the first person to find himself half way down a one-way street, going in the wrong direction, we know exactly how he felt. It must have been a lot harder to back a horse and carriage half a block than to back an automobile, not to mention the horse's loss of confidence in your ability to read signs.

18 Antonio Stradivari (Stradivarius), the Italian violin-maker, died on December 18, 1737. There are several ways to determine whether a violin is a genuine

Stradivarius. One is to drop it on a hard surface, say cement, and listen carefully to the sound. Another is to bite it. If you can open your mouth wide enough, the violin may or may not be a Stradivarius, but you are probably Joe E. Brown. Still another excellent test is to leave it outside overnight. If you go out in the morning to inspect it, and it is gone, it is probably the genuine article. Any Stradivarius with a date on it after 1737 should be viewed with suspicion.

19 On December 19, 1732, Benjamin Franklin began publication of *Poor Richard's Almanac*. This is full of aphorisms and homely (some of them downright ugly) sayings, one of the latter being "It is hard for an empty sack to stand upright." (Hard? It's impossible.) Franklin was the inventor, among other things, of bifocals, and it is a wonder he didn't think of the epigram: "He who wears glasses shouldn't throw stones."

20 The pneumatic automobile tire was thought up by Alexander T. Brown and George F. Stillman of Syracuse, New York, on December 20, 1892. This is the

The pneumatic tire

kind of thing it takes two men to invent, first putting their heads together and then, with some difficulty, getting them apart. The pneumatic tire did not spring up full-blown. Until they got hold of a pump, Mr. Brown and Mr. Stillman alternated at the valve stem, using every ounce of their lung power. Before the pneumatic tire, be it noted, tires were metal, wood, or solid rubber, and punctures and blow-outs were unheard of.

21 The Pilgrims first set foot on American soil at Plymouth, Massachusetts, on December 21, 1620. Fortunately, the first foot was set on a Rock, which was much easier to preserve than a spot on the sand. Recognizing at once its Historical Significance, and wishing to keep it from being chipped away for souvenirs, the Pilgrims put an iron fence around it, and across the street established their first commercial venture, a Gift Shoppe. That first boatload of Puritans was handicapped in one way. None of them could boast, "My ancestors came over on the *Mayflower*."

Winter is supposed to last from around December 21 to about March 21, or in other words (words which we have never quite understood) from the winter solstice to the vernal equinox. On December 21 or 22 the sun enters Capricorn, the tenth sign of the zodiac, represented by a figure which is part goat and part fish, a combination you don't come upon every day.

22 On December 22, 1944, General Anthony McAuliffe, commander of the 101st Airborne Division, replied to the German demand for his surrender at Bastogne with the celebrated retort, "Nuts!" When they heard about it, military commanders all over the world said enviously, "I wish I had thought of that." It is the shortest entry in *Bartlett's Familiar Quotations*, which maintains that General McAuliffe uttered it on December 23. It was probably either December 22 or December 23, and not both, for the statement could hardly have been extended over two days, unless the general had quite a drawl.

23 Richard Arkwright, the English industrialist, was born on December 23, 1732. By inventing the cotton spinning-frame, he helped along the Industrial Revolution and caused thousands of people to leave their back-breaking labor on the farm and take up back-breaking labor in the factory. Workers sitting all day hunched over Arkwright's spinning-frame dreamt at night that they were spiders. Were they glad to wake up! (Well, were they, with a twelve-hour day in the factory ahead of them?)

Dreamed they were spiders

The first Chinese theater was opened in San Francisco on December 23, 1852. A sign, "Celestial John," was over the entrance, though some thought it should be on the door to the men's room.

24 On December 24, 1949, the song "Rudolph, the Red-Nosed Reindeer" was sweeping the nation. For depth of feeling and for understanding of the true significance of Christmas, surely it can be compared with "All I Want for Christmas Is My Two Front Teeth" and that other lovely Christmas carol, "I Saw Mother Kissing Santa Claus."

25 Sir Isaac Newton, discoverer of the fact that apples fall from trees if they are not picked, was born on December 25, 1642. This British scientist made some interesting experiments with prisms, one of which led him to write the famous line, "Stone walls do not a prism make." He also stated the laws of motion, the most important of which is: "Moving bodies keep moving until they stop." It is not true that Newton had a son named Fig.

26 The coffee percolator was displayed to an eager world by James Nason, of Franklin, Massachusetts, on December 26, 1865. Mr. Nason was fully aware that the coffee thus brewed was no better than that prepared in an ordinary pot, but he knew everyone would be as fascinated as he by the sight of the coffee bubbling up into the glass top. As the percolator proved, a watched pot, or at least the liquid in it, *does* boil.

On December 26–27, 1947, 25.8 inches of snow fell in New York City. This was 4.9 inches more than fell in the famous Blizzard of 1888. But the 1947 snowstorm was not classified as a blizzard by the Weather Bureau, which can be stubborn about this sort of thing. Also, it had forecast "Clear and warmer" and kept hoping nobody would notice.

27 It was on December 27, 1900, that Carry Nation started her crusade against liquor by raiding a saloon in Wichita, Kansas. Patrons who were alarmed when she stormed in with a hatchet in her hand were relieved when she merely hacked at bottles, and sheepishly got up from the floor. Before she left, wading out through ankle-deep spirits, she threw a barrage of glasses and ash trays at a painting of an unclad lady over the bar, the name of which was subsequently changed to "Nude with Pock Marks."

28 Chewing gum was invented by William F. Semple, of Mount Vernon, Ohio, on December 28, 1869. The patent, which was strictly honest, referred to "a combination of rubber with other articles." Semple left it to others to figure out where to hide and how to retrieve the stuff, methods of scraping it off the sole of your shoe while standing on one leg, and how to chew, in polite society, with the mouth closed and no cracking or slurping. Chewing gum came to be a sure way of identifying Americans abroad, and was a great boon to baseball players who were not up to tobacco but wanted to appear professional. Since they chewed a whole package at a time, to make it look like a cud of tobacco, they in turn were a great boon to the chewing-gum industry. With his profits, gum-maker P. K. Wrigley bought a baseball club, known as the Chicago Spearmints.

29 The first nautical almanac was published in Boston on December 29, 1782. The present almanac, we blush to say, is a little salty in spots, but we hope no one has been offended. This is as good a place as any to drop the information, which has been burdening us for some time, that the word "almanac" comes from the Arabic *al*, the, and *manākh*, climate, weather. We could just as easily have filled these pages with information about tides, changes of the moon, eclipses, church festivals, and the like, and no doubt many readers would have found it more entertaining. But it is too late now, with only a couple of days to go. If you want to know about the weather, go outdoors and take a look.

30 Rasputin, the power behind the Russian throne, was assassinated on or about December 30, 1916. The date given by various authorities ranges from December 16 to December 31, probably because Rasputin was a tough customer whom it took a couple of weeks to put away. Known as the "Mad Monk" and the "Holy Devil," he was really a Holy Terror. He is reputed to have had a hold over the Czarina, possibly a half nelson or a hammerlock.

31 In England and Scotland this is Hogmanay, a celebration marking the end of the year, when children go around ringing doorbells and are given cakes if they make themselves scarce. After the rich food of the Christmas season, this usually finishes them off, and adults get a little peace and quiet. Happy Hogmanay! In the United States there is dining and dancing and revelry all evening. Then, at the stroke of twelve, all who are still on their feet "ring out the old and ring in the new." This is accomplished with horns and noisemakers that toot and rattle and do almost everything, it must be admitted, but ring. With the singing of "Auld Lang Syne" (or moving of the lips by those who can't remember, or never knew, the words), the year, like this book, comes to an

END.

Happy Hogmanay

About the Author

Richard Armour, who in this curious chronicle has done the greatest violence to the calendar since Julius Caesar, is well known to the many thousands of happy readers of his books, of which this is the twenty-second. A graduate of Pomona College and a Ph.D. from Harvard, he has held research fellowships in England and France, has taught at the University of Texas, Northwestern University, Wells College, the University of Freiburg, and the University of Hawaii, and is now Dean of the Faculty and Professor of English at Scripps College, in Claremont, California. Though he has written scholarly works of biography and literary criticism, he is best known for his books of humor and satire and the numerous pieces of light verse and prose which he has contributed to a wide variety of magazines. This is the seventh of his books to be illustrated by Campbell Grant, a versatile and widely acclaimed artist and illustrator who lives in Carpinteria, California.